HACKER ZONE

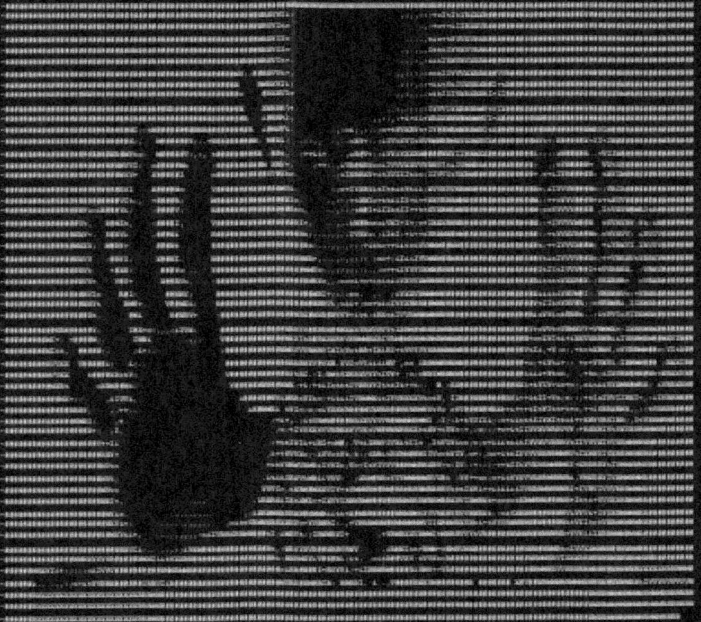

STEPHEN E.J RYAN

```
You are entering the Zone →


**The Hacker Zone**

sys→ login friend
sys→ password
sys→ **********

Welcome Friend
Welcome to the Hacker Zone....

zone→ DOWNLOAD "dystopia"
```

Rise up my sons and daughters!

Don the white hats and take your finger tips to war.

We ride to the battlefield upon which the battalions of black hats await us. It is time for your inner children to stand up and be counted. Time to come out of those bunkers and use your minds in actively constructive ways. Time to cast away the hours in useless pursuit, of watching the television and playing video games.

It is time to join the crusade against evil and to take up your computers to wage war against those who would steal your freedom and threaten the future of mankind.

Be not afraid of standing with us friends.

Cibermole

HACKER ZONE

Intrench Media

email: steve@intrench.com

Copyright @ 2021 Stephen E.J Ryan

No part of this book may be reproduced in any form without permission from the publisher.

Cover and illustrations in ASCII

Printed and bound by

Intrench Media

Paranoid fiction, Parody, Rhapsody, Menippean satire, Simulation Theory.

The Hacker Zone

www.thehackerzone.com

ISBN 0-000000-0-0

HACKER ZONE

**AND HOW THEY PLAN
TO SET HUMANITY FREE!**

Dedication

In,
Memory of the guys
who never made it through the breakdown
(R.I.P)

To,
All the White Hats
who value independence, freedom and truth
above all things.

To,
Everyone who cared

+

And To the
Black Hats

Shame on YOU!

A CIA SUSPECT?

OR A TARGET FOR A HAIRCUT? OLIE 2005?

We are all like the hacker

Each and everyone of us has at one time or other moved like the hacker!

Whether our target be a member of the family, friends, acquaintances, fellow employees, strangers or things.

Whether our motive was good or bad.
Biased or impartial, matters not.

The Truth is …
When our emotions overpower us….

WE BEGIN TO HACK!

Hacker Cell is….

Noah:[healer]
{hydra-2343-kills}

Sykes:[engineer]
{hydra-6243-kills}

Smouth:[navigator]
{hydra-3020-kills}

Jaqs:[messenger]
{hydra-190-kills}

Cibermole:[spymaster]
{hydra-8033-kills}

From: **Noah** (White Hat)
To: **All Readers of Hacker Cell**
Subject: **Prepare to defend the human spirit**

When the finger tips of the black hat crack across the keyboard you can be sure they are unleashing their sinister droid signatures on an unsuspecting target.

These evil knights march against the great and the good in the name of the predatory race that reigns in the underworld we all call the Internet.

Yes…these faceless demons have sought out yet another medium upon which they can unite to control the lives of ordinary men and women.

To manipulate their minds, to steal their souls, to hijack their future and in so doing make you bow down before them and serve their twisted agenda.

Yes my friends, be not under any illusion that the dark ones wish fear and poverty upon you. Be not naïve enough to think that they seek your presence for any kind and honorable cause. For they are the sons and daughters of satan and you must fight them with every ounce of your will.

In the name of FREEDOM.

Prepare to fight to defend your liberty.

Prepare to fight for your lives!

Noah.

From: **Sykes** (White Hat)
To: **All Readers of Hacker Cell**
Subject: **With mind tools we fight**

We scan with our minds
We construct tools with our minds
We attack with our minds
We defend with our minds
We retreat with our minds
We love with our minds
So we might set humanity free

Sykes.

From: **Smouth** (White Hat)
To: **All Readers of Hacker Cell**
Subject: **Look hard and you will find your destiny**

They said to me, you must do everything we say.
You must do everything we do.
Everything, in everyway, just like us.
Then one day they cast me aside.
I was too much for them to handle.
Too disruptive.

What I thought of as my life, was suddenly taken away from me forever.
Everyone and everything lost forever.
Smashed into a billion pieces, which could never be put back together again.
Never to be the same again.
With only myself to blame.

It was some years later that I was able to accept what had happened and to start the process of looking for a new identity.
Looking for a new purpose in my life.

Once you start looking, its often the thing you are seeking, that finds you.

It was then I was found
It was then I found my calling
It was then I knew what my life would be spent doing

I had found my destiny
As a white hat united against tyranny
Smouth.

From: **Jaqs** (White Hat)
To: **All Readers of Hacker Cell**
Subject: **How I became a computer hacker**

There was a time when I had no real purpose in my life. When there seemed no reason to go to school. No reason to work hard, no reason to get out of bed in the morning. No point to doing anything at all really, except hang around and disrupt other people all day.

Yeah, that was my calling. To do nothing, but disrupt!

Then one day something came in to my life that changed me forever. Something that was so intensely exciting that I was willing to give up my bad ways and turn them into something really cool.

That something was computer hacking.

Sure, I'd thought about doing stuff like this before, but only for reasons that would have got me locked up.

But I'd never really thought about computer hacking for any other reason. For any good reason!

It was then that my life changed forever.

The day I first met Professor Albamall and began to understand what it means to be a white hat computer hacker.

Jaqs.

Foreword

There are two types of hacker in this world.
The white hats and the black hats!

Guess who the guys are with the good motive? Guess who the guys are fighting to rid the world of evil, bringing freedom to all?

White hat hacking is the art of designing computer tools, techniques, strategies, concepts, exploits and counter-methods to attack and defend against a bad guy on the Internet. It is the art of mounting covert operations, spying and corrupting the evil black hat movement. The art of using the creative mind to see beyond the obvious, to envision possibilities way beyond that of the average computer user.

Anyone can become a white hat. Anyone! Not anyone can be the best athlete or a brain surgeon, but anyone can become a white hat. It means in reality that anyone can become an artist, because that is what white hat hackers are. They are skilled craftsmen that through their hands and minds create powerful online expressions that help save peoples lives. In fact I would go to say that they will become the Galileo's, the Einstein's, the Da Vinci's of their day, only they will become even greater.

They are the artists who have the most remarkable of all missions. To rid the world of evil and bring freedom to all through their work. What artist of yesterday, today or tomorrow will truly be able to say they had such power to move hearts and minds of whole nations away from evil and tyranny towards good and moral behaviour? The white hat hacker is truly going to have an impact on what we know today as art. White hats are going to give new meaning to art that will not be accepted by the establishment, yet will not be able to be denied by it either.

The value of such art will be there for all to see and those who produce it will know that their lives were well spent. They will know that their lives really meant something and that the evidence of their endeavours is there for all to see.

Their inventions will remain long after they have left this planet.

In an Internet world that is constantly changing the white hat hacker seeks one thing above all things.

"Intrenchment of the target".

The white hat hacker seeks to bring people together everywhere, to make possible sustainable relationships built upon confidence and trust. The white hat hacker seeks to orchestrate developing the very best conditions on the Internet and ensuring they are sustainable for all time. To "fix firmly and securely" the conditions of good and to break the stranglehold of evil. To rid the world of pain and suffering caused by ignorance and fear, instigated by the devious minded. Those oppressors of freedom. White hats seek to address the balance of good against evil, by destroying fear-corrupted ignornant spaces on the Internet and replacing them with love and righteousness.

INTRENCHED FOR ALL TIME.

Such is the power of love!

Rise up my sons and daughters. Don the white hats and take your finger tips to war. We ride to the battlefield upon which the battalions of black hats await us. It is time for your inner children to stand up and be counted. Time to come out of those bunkers and use your minds in actively constructive ways. Time to cast away the hours in useless pursuit, of watching the television and playing video games. It is time to join the crusade against evil and to take up your computers to wage war against those who would steal your freedom and threaten the future of mankind.

Be not afraid of standing with us friends.

Join with us! Join with us!

Cibermole.

BOOK OUTLINE

<u>Introduction – Freedom Fighters</u>　　- (Page 5)
Hacker Zone
Visual Mind Prison
Black Hat Cult
Freedom Fighters

<u>Chapter 1 – Meet Jaqs</u>　　- (page 13)
About Me
The Diskette
Hacker Bible
Hackers Mission

<u>Chapter 2 – Team Cibermole</u>　　-(page 21)
Profile of a Hacker Cell
Sykes
Smouth
Noah
Cibermole
Jaqs

<u>Chapter 3 – Hacker World</u>　　-(page 33)
DROIDS
Programmers
Handlers
Landscape
Movement
Other Worlds
Security
Intrenchment
Zonelessness

Chapter 4 – Hacker Behaviour   -(page 45)
Composers
Engagers
Enablers
Exploiters
Intrenchers

Chapter 5 – Enemy Behaviour   -(page 53)
Predatory Minds
Dark Strategies
Deadly Posture

Chapter 6 – Hacker Training   -(page 61)
Body Training
Behaviour Training
Learning Training
Intelligence Training
Battle Training
Cause Training

Chapter 7 – Hacker Techniques   -(page 73)
Covert Operations
Creative Visualisation
Intelligence Acquisition
Attack Strategies
Defence Strategies

BOOK OUTLINE

<u>Chapter 8 – Hacker Tools</u>   - (page 83)
Proteon
Scanners
Transparent and Private Speak
Black Magic
Psychological Operations
Social Engineering

<u>Chapter 9 – Hack Anatomy</u>   - (page 95)
Defined
Adventure
Target Model
Hack Types – Threat
Hack Types – Opportunity

<u>Chapter 10 – Hack Example</u>   - (page 105)
Tomb of the Game Testers
Summary
Beginning
Middle
End

<u>Chapter 11 – Threat Network</u>   - (page 112)
Perpertrators
Bugs (threat level 1)
Virus (threat level 2)
DROIDS/Handlers (threat level 3)
RealWorld Agents (threat level 4)
Alien Masters (threat level 5)

Chapter 12 – Visual Mind Prison   -(page 124)
Attention
Concentration
Identity
Reality
Freedom

Chapter 13 – Black Hat Cult   -(page 134)
Pyramidians
Plot
Raptorialis
Vulnerabilities

Chapter 14 – White Hat Bible   -(page 142)
I_Atom
I_Factor
I_Motive
I_Model
I_Exploit
I_Hacker

Chapter 15 – Hydra Hackers   -(page 154)
Spirit
Movement
Attack
Exit

BOOK OUTLINE

<u>Chapter 8 – Hacker Tools</u>　　　　　- (page 83)
Proteon
Scanners
Transparent and Private Speak
Black Magic
Psychological Operations
Social Engineering

<u>Chapter 9 – Hack Anatomy</u>　　　　- (page 95)
Defined
Adventure
Target Model
Hack Types – Threat
Hack Types – Opportunity

<u>Chapter 10 – Hack Example</u>　　　- (page 105)
Tomb of the Game Testers
Summary
Beginning
Middle
End

<u>Chapter 11 – Threat Network</u>　　　- (page 112)
Perpertrators
Bugs (threat level 1)
Virus (threat level 2)
DROIDS/Handlers (threat level 3)
RealWorld Agents (threat level 4)
Alien Masters (threat level 5)

Chapter 12 – Visual Mind Prison   -(page 124)
Attention
Concentration
Identity
Reality
Freedom

Chapter 13 – Black Hat Cult   -(page 134)
Pyramidians
Plot
Raptorialis
Vulnerabilities

Chapter 14 – White Hat Bible   -(page 142)
I_Atom
I_Factor
I_Motive
I_Model
I_Exploit
I_Hacker

Chapter 15 – Hydra Hackers   -(page 154)
Spirit
Movement
Attack
Exit

GUIDE TO HOW WHITE HATS PLAN TO SET HUMANTY FREE

WHAT THE VOICES SAID IN MY HEAD

Introduction:	FREEDOM FIGHTERS	Jaqs
Chapter1:	MEET JAQS	Jaqs
Chapter2:	TEAM CIBERMOLE	Jaqs
Chapter3:	HACKER WORLD	Jaqs
Chapter4	HACKER BEHAVIOUR	Smouth
Chapter5:	ENEMY BEHAVIOUR	Cibermole
Chapter6:	HACKER TRAINING	Noah
Chapter7:	HACKER TECHNIQUES	Jaqs
Chapter8:	HACKER TOOLS	Sykes
Chapter9:	ANATOMY OF A HACK	Smouth
Chapter10:	EXAMPLE OF A HACK	Jaqs
Chapter11:	THREAT NETWORK	Cibermole
Chapter12:	VISUAL MIND PRISON	Noah
Chapter13:	BLACK HAT CULT	Cibermole
Chapter14:	WHITE HAT BIBLE	Noah
Chapter15:	HYDRA HACKERS	Hacker Cell
Appendix I:	TERMINOLOGY	
Appendix II:	WHO FUELS THE MATRIX	
Appendix III:	BIBLIOGRAPHY	

THANKS TO THE VOICES FOR THEIR CONTRIBUTION
IN THE MAKING OF THIS BOOK. I THINK.

Introduction – Freedom Fighters – *by Jaqs*

Hacker Zone

You think talking about hacking is easy?
It's actually quite difficult for all sorts of reasons. No bigger reason than the risk I run at revealing the secrets I know.
5 years undercover working against every crank and gangster on the Internet has taught me more than most so called security experts would ever learn in a lifetime. You see, to catch the worst kinds of criminal you need to think the same way they do. You need to become what they are in order for you to have any chance of defeating them.
In short, you need to get in the Zone. The Hacker Zone.

Sure you'll read all sorts of books about hacking and you'll even learn a trick or two, but to be the best you need to think like the best. No university degree, no privileged background, no amount of money can make you smarter. You could be the biggest Hollywood actor, an international football star or even the President of the USA and you still won't come close to the levels of power and intelligence that a growing number of hackers are accumulating. As the world becomes ever more wired the power of the hacker grows by an order of magnitude and ordinary citizens find themselves increasingly vulnerable to dark and sinister forces which they are unable to control and see. There are other reasons why speaking out is difficult. Hackers are explorers. We are driven by our curiosity to know more. To go where others have never trodden before. To solve problems in totally unconventional ways and to conquer and challenge everything that stands in our way. Which means that when I'm talking to you, I'm not doing the things I love the most, like being in the Zone? It's quite un-natural for me to sit down, recall what happened to me in the past and actually play it back to you in speech. I leave the Zone simply because I know that this is the only way to get some very important messages out to you.

YOU'VE BEEN HACKED! NO TRACE LEFT

```
            You are entering the Zone →


                **The Hacker Zone **



jaq→ Login jaqs
jaq→ Password
jaq→ **********

Welcome Jaqs
Welcome to the hacker Zone....

Zone→_
```

Visual Mind Prison

So why contact you at all? Why reach out to readers everywhere with tales that will frighten you, with images that are largely hidden from you at the moment? Why drag up the bad things that have happened on the Internet in the past and hold them up for all to see?

To begin to explain, you first need to know that there are two types of hacker. The evil predator guys who are trying to take control of you through the Internet and those fighting to protect you from their evil.
The first type of hackers are known as black hats and the second type, white hats.

In the early days, the Internet was largely controlled by the military and educational establishments. There were more white hats exploring and patrolling the Internet in those days. As the 70's, 80's and 90's came and went, the number of "white hats" fell away and the "black hats" began to swell in number. Many of the white hats went to work for companies like Microsoft, Cisco and IBM who are in the business of making the computers, the networks and the software that is the foundation of the Internet today.
Unfortunately when the white hats disappeared inside these organizations it became increasingly difficult for them to play a useful role in combating the growing number of black hat hackers who were busy carrying out their evil deeds in every part of the globe. Those of us who were still on the outside were left to face the wrongdoers or flee for our lives. My friends and I stayed on to fight alongside groups based in other countries around the world. Most of us stayed loyal to the cause to fight for freedom, to explore and to defend. Some however were lured over to the dark side by promises of fame and fortune.
Some even became trapped inside the Visual Mind Prison.

Select →
1----Visual Mind Prison
------------WWW
------------TV
------------Radio
------------Mobile
------------Games
------------Adults
<ctrl-c> -----Command Line (hackers this way)

(Leave the Mind Prison behind – LIVE LIFE AT THE COMMAND LINE)

```
Welcome to the prison

The Visual Mind Prison

#############
#  \   ##   /  #
#   \  ##  /   #
#############
#   /  ##  \   #
#  /   ##   \  #
#############

Login to the WWW mind prison
http:\\www.yaayeyyee.com\booboo\junkjunk

(Walk this way to the black hat trap)
LET YOUR MIND BECOME STOLEN FOR ALL TIME
```

Black Hat Cult

What made me first think of writing to you was when I finally realized that the battle had been lost. When it became clear that the Internet had been lost to the black hats. I thought about the prospect of people becoming more and more dependent on the Internet to carryout their basic daily needs. For buying food, for managing their money, for education and for health. I thought about what it was like over the past 30 years and what it is like today.....and then I thought about how the future might look. A future where we were all dependent on technology in order to survive..... Worst still, I thought about a future where we were all held to ransom by the black hats and had to live our lives as slaves to people who only ever had one motive.............

"To control mankind for their own selfish ends."

And there is only one way to protect you....that is to alert you to this problem and to help you to understand the type of people and methods you will be up against in the future. Whether you are a hacker or an ordinary citizen, you need to know that there are sinister forces at work on the Internet. You really ought to start preparing to face them in the future.
Black hats are people from all walks of life. Some of them are bus drivers, some are politicians and some are even people in the church. They are sworn to secrecy so you would never know who they were. In the early days the black hats were just a disorganised band of mercenaries operating in different parts of the world.
Today the black hats are an international organisation with a well thought out agenda to take over the planet and they intend to achieve this by using the Internet to control everyone and everything.
To control YOU!

```
                    CULT OF THE BLACK HATS
           (THE PYRAMID SYMBOL AND THE ALL SEEING EYE)
                               .
                            \ - /
                             (@)*
                            *_* *
                          *  o  *   *
                         *  *  *  *    *
                        /_____\      *
                       * * *     * *      *
                      * * *       * *    /
                     * * *         * *  /
                    * * *           * */
                   * * *             * */
                  ******************* */
                  -------------------
```

```
captain scarlet up
captain scarlet looking for victims <ctrl-C>
switching to exploit mode

Zone→ scan targets 122.300.303.000 - 099
target 122.300.303.033 has severe weaknesses

Zone→ scan target 122.300.303.033
2 computers found <fred> <John>

Zone→ trash <fred> + <John> ← RANDOM EXPLOIT
computers <fred> and >John> successfully trashed
(damage) = <fred> corrupted hard drive;
<john> deployed trojan virus to pass private email
    messages to <Capn>

Zone→ hide captain scarlet
all evidence of exploits cleared for captain scarlet
```

Freedom Fighters

When you type on your keyboard, beware that your keystrokes are not being intercepted and recorded by someone else on the outside. Beware that your passwords are not being stolen and your files being infected by parasites and insidious viruses. Beware that your time online is not being monitored by evil trojan programs and your identity being acquired for use elsewhere in the world.

Ever thought what it must be like to write a letter and have it altered by someone else, only to find that your words had been turned into gobble-de-gook? To have your personal email messages automatically forwarded to everyone on the Internet or to have filthy words inserted and scrawled across your website. Such are the acts of the black hats. But there is much worse and you will learn of it as you read through this manuscript.

So there you have it. The Internet is under attack. You yourself will be under attack in the future. Your own children, friends and colleagues will be under attack. You need to get smart. To read everything you can about the Internet and to learn the tools, techniques and ways of the white hat hacker. Only then will you be prepared for what is to come in the future. You must join the growing army of folks out there who are preparing for battle with the demons of the technological revolution. This is a call to arms. Join with us in the war against the evil doers! Most of all, you must learn how to develop the mind of a hacker. Only then will you truly be in a position to take your place in the ranks of the good and the courageous. Only then will you be equipped with the intellectual and creative tools to outsmart the enemy. Only then will you have a worthwhile cause in which to fight - for the rest of your natural lives.
"Login to the Zone and fight in the name of Freedom".

HACKER CELL Are: →

Jaqs
Cibermole
Smouth
Noah
Sykes

```
Zone→ whois [ONLINE]

 HACKER CELL            vs.          HACKMASTERS

*White Hats*             |            *Black Hats*
                         |
Jaq_                     |            hackM_
CM_                      |            VirNerd_
Smo_                     |            capn_
Noa_                     |
Syk_                     |

Online Now_____

Zone→ whois [hackM]
<hackM> is the handle for a black hat in Chicago>
|||||||||||||||||||||||||||||||||||||||||||||||||
Zone→ whois [Jaq]
<Jaq_ is the handle for a member of a white
 hat cell based in London, England, UK>
|||||||||||||||||||||||||||||||||||||||||||||||||
```

Chapter 1 – Meet Jaqs – *by Jaqs*

About Me

I was raised by my parents, with my two sisters, Susan and Julie. Up to 1997 I was educated oversees in South Africa, but then I went to school in England. By the age of 17 I had saved up enough money to buy my first PC.

In 1998 going under the handle of Jaqs I entered and won a computer competition which was organised by someone I had looked up to for many years, the late Professor Albamall. The Professor passed away in 2001, under very suspicious circumstances. At the time of winning the competition I was extremely excited and later in June 1998 I received my prize through the post. I opened the envelope which had been well bound and inside found a letter from the Professor congratulating me on my success, together with an old 3.5 inch diskette.

The most astonishing thing of all was when I inserted and loaded the disk and found myself being transported inside the Internet. LOL…Ok! So I must be a lunatic right??
Can you imagine seeing me disappear though my computer screen, inside the computer, down the telephone wires and into a world run by networks? What we are talking about here is not being physically transported inside the Internet, but about entering a transcendental state, a kind of dream world where you mentally enter a different dimension in which you can operate more effectively.

This space between our real physical world and the virtual world of the Internet is called "The Zone". Only the smartest hackers are able to enter "The Zone" and carryout their work from there.
Think about it. From within the Zone, you can see the physical world where we all live and you can see …………..
Virtual World,
…Where the technology wars are taking place!

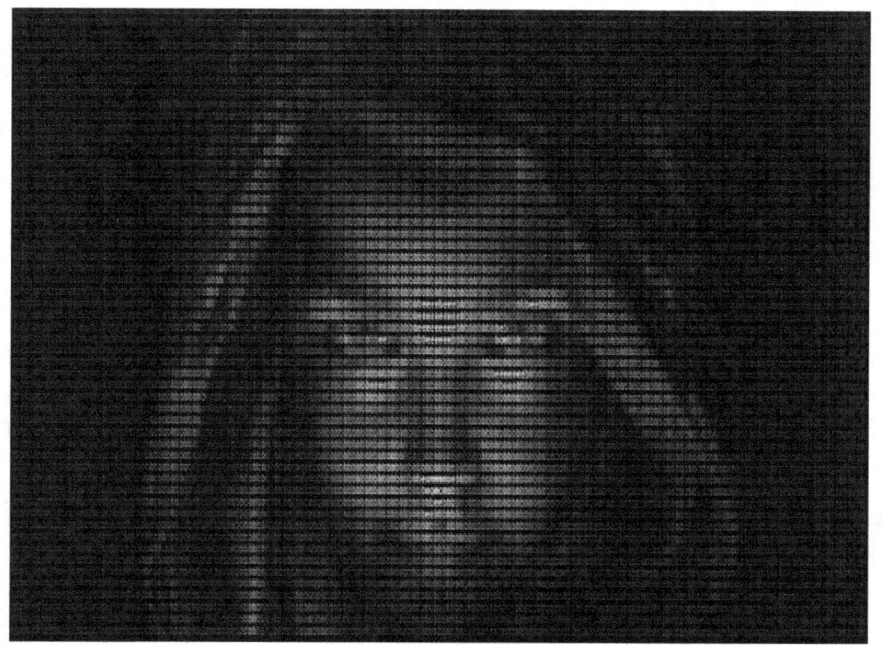

I can see on both sides of the ZONE!

I am the Messenger

I am Jaqs Carter

The Diskette

The diskette the Professor had sent me contained all the instructions I needed to prepare myself for entering the Zone. There were instructions on how to scan the Internet for new information on the whereabouts and activities of the "black hats". Instructions on how to defend computer systems when under attack and for understanding the multitude of techniques used by the wrong doers. Professor Albamall had even taken the time to provide instructions on how to prepare my mind and body for switching channel into Hacker Zone. The professor's letter read like this:

Dear "Jaqs",
You are the winner of the Professor Albamall prize for aspiring hackers. You won this competition because the answers you gave to our questions meant that you have shown the greatest aptitude for hacking out of all the candidates selected to take the exam.

Hackers are people who solve problems creatively at the same time as challenging conventional thinking. The security of the Internet is paramount to the survival of the human race in the future. Those who seek to undermine humanity through the Internet do not think in conventional ways. They do not perpetrate their evil deeds in ways that can be easily picked up by security specialists. In order to combat this scourge we need to recruit people who have minds that are capable of out-thinking the "black hats".
To this end I invite you to join an elite group of hackers codenamed 'Hacker Cell'. You will be known as the Messenger. There are further instructions on the enclosed diskette and you will be contacted in due course by one of the team.
Well done and good luck in the future.
Yours Truly,
Professor C. Albamall

```
Loading Zone Diskette.........


Prof. A - Hack Competition Winner 1998
Handle: Jaqs; "The Messenger"

Select the Menu item
1.    Hack Tools
2.    Hack Techniques
3.    Hacker ZONE (Preparation for)
4.    Scanners & Mobile Devices Unleashed
5.    Black Hat Threats Uncovered
6.    White Hat Bible

Jaq:\ 1 <enter>
```

Hackers Bible

Six months prior to his death the Professor had called me to meet him where he handed me a diskette which he said contained a library of over 10,000 hacks, which he told me to use with the utmost care and respect.

All his working life had been spent living the life of a ...White Hat...... Yes, every company he worked for, every person he met, every problem he solved had been carried out with the motivation of the white hat hacker.

He fought for a good cause. He used his hacker brain to defeat evil and maintain freedom for all. He met all kinds of people in all kinds of difficult places.

He told me that he once worked in an electronics lab building medical robots and founded a computer company designing Internet software. He worked in all sorts of places and as alias Professor Albamall built many relationships with elite hackers from New York to London and beyond.

Think about it, 25 years working in every type of situation, in every type of position, dealing with every type of difficult problem. Don't you think he would learn a lot? Don't you think the mind of the hacker would understand even more than that of non-hackers, because his mind was constantly active?

Constantly scanning for black hats! Looking for new ways to solve problems, to cut to the chase, to make things better than they were before.

What the Professor had handed to me was more than white hat magicians tricks and special hack powers.

It was a Hackers Bible. The most special of all guides.

PASSAGE FROM HACKER BIBLE - Purpose

What strange existence is this that we carry each other to the ends of the earth, only to part company!

Evaporating into the air, the soil and the seas? Where did we start, why did we, what for?

Some men strive for everything and some men strive for nothing. All are essentially the same, by their own mortality. As vast swathes of beings tread this planet, generation upon generation, moment after moment, move after move.

What does each and every one of us reap?

Ask not what we reap - but what we sow? For it is the spirit of man that recognises the futility of life, but that walking towards the sunset finally realises that life means nothing more than one mans journey for another. If he does not believe in God, then let him believe that his life is of no value unless it is lived in service to mankind. Not because it is written, not because it is right, but because there is nothing else!
PEOPLE ARE CERTAINLY WORTH FIGHTING FOR

Hackers Mission

The Diskette was entitled.
"To contribute to the lessening of the sea of tears that surrounds humanity".

This became my mission. This became my cause.

Ever since that time I have sailed from the bottom to the top in my life, then sunk to the bottom and picked myself up again. But one thing has always remained constant - my determination to make a real difference and to rid this world of ignorance and fear so that every man and woman might live their lives in peace and harmony. So this white hat has a serious mission and any one that gets in my way, better watch out! If you're a black hat, then take care because this white hat is on your tail and you are likely to get your teeth kicked in!

You just can't be a white hat because you know how to write computer programs. There has to be a good cause behind what you do. White hats fight for many good causes, but it mostly comes down to one thing. Defeat evil and free the world from the tyranny of others. Use the mind of the creative, the inspired, the innovator, the technologist, to solve problems for now and for all time.
It's time to begin the journey inside the Internet. It's time to use the knowledge of over 1 million missions in the lives of 10,000 white hats living around the world.
Time to experience the ways, methods and techniques of the white hat hacker. To discover the kinds of evil deed that happen on the Internet each day and to begin to decide whether you are best suited to becoming a white hat yourself. Whatever you do in your life. Take care that you do the things you think worthwhile and lead you toward freedom.

PASSAGE FROM HACKER BIBLE - Justice
He, who sees through the veil of illusion, watches the truth in all its glory. This man moves towards the truth and will always be on firm ground.

Man must seek the truth, the causes, and the motives. Strive to understand at every point the facts, the meaning and the value of any one thing.

Waste no time with illusions of effects of events. Spend your time wisely considering only those things that move you toward the truth. Only then will there be any basis for freedom.

| Chapter 2 – Team Cibermole – *by Jaqs* |

Profile of a Hacker Cell

The black hats have been trying to shut us up for years in order to thwart our efforts at repelling their evil and to prevent us from telling what we know. As the years have gone by they have grown stronger and stronger and we weaker and weaker, as the sheer number of them has increased as more and more people come online.

Few have made it to this stage, some have passed away, some have crossed over to the other side and some have simply vanished into thin air. But there is no doubt that the white hat column forming the guardian wall around humanity is standing firm, albeit under ferocious attack.

Before Professor Albamall died he told me to learn the battles of the past so that I could use this knowledge in action in the future. He invited me to join the battle against the black hats and said it was a call to arms.

Before that time I'd had no direction in my life and the things I wanted to do like hacking were things that were not seen as legitimate and honourable practices.

Professor Albamall made me feel like I had a place to belong, an identity, a purpose for being alive. Some direction even. Now I had something to look back on when I was old and say, "That was me! I was an hacker, one of the best, part of an elite anti-hacker cell helping to make the Internet a safer place for everyone". "I was a White Hat!"

So what did joining up actually involve? Well I have to say this was the strangest of all experiences because you don't officially join anything. In fact I have been a member of the same hacker cell for 7 years and have never once met any of the other members.

It is difficult to calculate just how many white hats there are in the world given our cause is fought by many who never disclose who they are. Hacker Cell is a tiny group of elite hackers belonging to the white hat order. In our cell, there are five members. Cibermole, Sykes, Smouth, Noah and me.

You have to remember that behind every predator and parasite on the Internet, there is a physical body to which it belongs.
Some of these people will use the dirtiest of online tricks and will even stoop so low as to attack your homes and even your family. Even to the extent of stealing your identity, rendering you empty and useless before all men.
We need to be extremely careful that our personal details are never disclosed to anyone, not even to the other members of the group. It is difficult to defend those who are the targets of the black hats - if we ourselves can be personally identified.
We decide who can be trusted based on past behaviour in battle. I've been with the gang for 7 years and have attended over 200 missions against the black hats and through these wars I have built the utmost respect for everyone in the team. Even though I don't know who they really are.
Each of us has an alias name and we use ASCII based symbols to construct a unique gamer tag. My own handle is Jaqs and I have used this since the time I was first invited to become a member of the white hats by the greatest hacker of all time, Professor Albamall.
We only ever communicate online using the ASCII symbol set, which is really just using text, like numbers and characters. We never use images, unless they are translated into ASCII. We believe that the most basic form of expression is best, because we prefer to talk straight without introducing complexity. If messages cannot be said using simple terms, then they shouldn't be said at all.
It is said that a picture can tell a thousand stories, our view is,
"We never want to tell one thousand stories…"
"We only ever want to tell one at a time!"

Sykes (our engineer)

Don't judge people by their identity - you need to judge them by their actions. You can't say he is a good guy because he says he is or looks that way. You need to see him behave that way and probably for some time before you can begin to trust him!

Hacker Cell is a formidable force.

I know this, not by what they say they can do – but by what I've seen them do in the past. This tells me that if everyone continues to keep their side of the bargain that we will always work well together in the future. It tells me that we fight for the same cause and that we all have useful talents and experience to offer. It tells me that my comrades are also willing to take risks in order to safeguard humanity from the predatory ones.

There are those who tell the world that they are the ones who created the Internet, when in fact it was thousands of engineers who built it. They say that they were the architects, when in fact the designers came from this same body of engineers. They say they are the real hackers when in fact they are just some people who got caught!

People who swapped their less than cosy life as teenage outcasts for million dollar mansions in Silicon Valley. There is no one special person, there are only those who got rich and had a voice to be able to say such things and then there are the engineers. Those who quietly work away at building systems. Building them because they love and care about their work, not because they seek to dominate others and get rich quick.

You know a good engineer when they say things like "this model won't sustain a simple attack once in the wild" or "whoever wrote this code weren't seeing the big picture" or "I'll reverse engineer the .exe, rather than re-design from scratch" or "we only have 3 hours and it will take me 6 to 7 hours to write a new engine – better run with what we got and adapt the code".

What is amazing about these guys is they actually do what they say. THEY ACTUALLY DO STUFF. THEY DON'T JUST SIT AROUND AND TALK ABOUT IT! THEY ACTUALLY DO STUFF! What gives them the edge is that they can build really competitive solutions to problems, on their own. How many people or even groups of people can say that today?

Our engineer is codenamed Sykes.

You think that computers are going to take control? Well think again! With guys like Sykes around mankind will always have an edge.

You want to get technical? You want to get really technical? How far can you push it? How far does it go? You want to build a space ship? You want to recreate the Internet? Redefine computer games - far beyond anything that you can buy in the shops today? You want to outsmart the side with the covert agenda? The side who are building the systems to take over the planet? You want to be one step ahead of them? Want to know about the future of technology? For good or for bad?

Our engineer is a technical artist. A minimalist designer. Someone who believes in producing effective architecture. Someone who dislikes window dressing.

As the beasts put into place their technology agenda and create the scams and botnets that will ultimately enslave us all, so we have sought to protect mankind against a takeover by the black hats. We know how the Internet works. We know how and when it moves. We understand its ingredients and that of the enemy. We see through the electronic illusion like an x-ray machine through a human being.

Our engineer is in tune with the materials and movements of the 4th technological revolution – and he is prepared to do intellectual battle at any technical level – in the name of truth, freedom and justice.

Smouth (our navigator)

It is no surprise that the predatory ones have chosen the Internet as the mechanism to take ultimate control of the planet. Connecting everything and everyone to the Internet means that the predators have a window in to your homes, your offices and your relationships with others.

Best part about it for them is that they can make this all happen without you ever noticing. Of course you don't notice. Do you really know what your computer is doing?

They also know that if you do get wise to what is going on that the Internet is so vast that you can easily get lost in the noise. So even if you expose what they're doing, people are going to think that you're an idiot, a crackpot and you will never be able to get enough good people to take notice of you to support your story.

Deception lies deep in the roots of the Internet and these black hats have spent billions of dollars creating a smoke screen to shield the real agenda from the people. Instead they re-direct the attention of humanity toward illusionary criminals – they call hackers!!! Their publicity denigrates the name of the hacker and seeks to confuse and trick people into believing that all hackers belong to one kind. The black hat kind! Well let me tell you that there is only one kind of hacker – the white hats. The other guys are certainly nothing like anything I've ever seen before (call them crackers, bushwhackers, thieves) ....I don't care.

They are not what hacking is all about!

No.... hacking has always been a noble art. It is the meaning of hacking that is being twisted and changed making it appear that we, the white hats, are the same as them. That we are devious minded criminals. Predators like them. These stories they tell serve their agenda well.

Well let me tell you – you filthy beasts!! We know you're out there. We know what cause you serve and we know where to find you. There is no tricking us. We see the signs, you cannot pull the wool over our eyes and you cannot frighten us.

For our navigator codenamed (Smouth) sees all. She detects your sinister games, your propaganda displays, your patterns of deception. She knows the pathways to evil, the tricks and the effects you create to move people to fear.

She knows you, she sees you, she feels you, she senses you, she tastes you, she smells you. She sees beyond the five senses in to the realms of the predatory ones. You can run, but you cannot hide. She is our all seeing eye and she is on our side. She fights on the side of the white hats.

SMOUTH - NAVIGATOR

Noah (our healer)

When all around you is lies, war and strife. When you are down to your last reserves of courage and conviction. When you feel that you can no longer take the strain anymore. Where does the relief come from?
Who is there to pick you up?

We, the fighters of freedom are intense in our duty to defeat the enemy. We direct our minds and bodies towards fighting fear and injustice. We give ourselves up utterly and completely to the challenge. But what of our souls? Who tends to these in the times when we are at our most vulnerable, at our most wearisome, at our most desperate?

There are times when we must seek counsel and there are times when we must be sought out by counsel. Times when we must be reminded of the path; that our cause is more worthy than our own needs and that whatever happens, that God will always be at our side in battle. This gives us renewed hope that all will be well and strength to continue in our quest.

Our healer is codenamed Noah and is the editor and keeper of the Hacker Bible, prepared over many decades by Professor Albamall. Noah is the monitor of us all. He watches our every move and keeps a careful eye that we remain true to the cause. In times of need Noah is the one who we turn to for wisdom. He is the one who heals us in the dark times – when we venture off the path toward illusion and when we lose sight of who we really are.

Noah is the one who brings light to the darkness. Relief to the pain. Hope to fear. He is the one that black hats fear the most because battles are not won by warriors and weapons alone. They are not won by the sword. They are won by appealing to the hearts and minds of the people and in so doing comrades will follow the cause to the ends of the earth.

It is true that Noah is the most feared because he sees war differently than the rest of us. He sees right to the heart of it. He gives us spirit to carry on when all appears lost.

They are right to fear him, for he is Gods disciple, the custodian of our cause. For he is the holder of the manuscript from which we draw insight to deliver humanity from evil.

The Power in the Motive

What is the difference between a hacker and a Not-hacker?

Is it that the hacker...
1. Knows more about technology
2. Knows more tricks
3. Knows more about black hats
4. Knows more about white hats
5. Knows more about coding

Well maybe, but could there be more to it than that?
Is is that...
They know the importance of right motive, right thinking and right action.

Yes,
Hacker power is about having right motive!
Hacker direction is about thinking the right thoughts!
Hacker delivery is about expressing right action! NOAH

Cibermole (our spymaster)

Outsiders can very rarely have great insight. Even those who can sense the direction of the enemy and envision the path they will take. Even those who have the capability of making use of such knowledge are limited in their powers.

An organisation like the black hats is not only covert and deceitful in the way it behaves, but its members also hold positions of influence and power at every level in society. To understand the dynamics of such an entity it is essential to be privy to intelligence about it.
Any such confidential information is only available to a small number of people, right at the top of the organisation.
You need to be a key player in the black hats or a highly trusted person in order to acquire this information. You need to be one of THE most trusted people to have insight into the global agenda on a daily basis.
You may have heard in the world of espionage of the term - mole. Similarly you may know the security term – trojan, mainly used in reference to computer viruses.

Well the fourth member of the gang codenamed Cibermole is both of these things. Cibermole is a highly trusted member of the black hat fraternity (but really a white hat). He is a mole in the enemy camp and has been working underground in the black hat community since he was only 16 years old. His job is to spy on the black hats and ensure that we are always informed of where the next attack is going to take place. His other job is to ensure that he causes as much disruption as possible to the black hat agenda from inside their organisation.
This is the tojan horse like role he plays.
He is programmed to self-destruct should his position ever become compromised. This situation in itself would cause untold damage, given it would result in the exposure of all of the key people and other beings at the top the pyramid.

Cibermole is a highly capable intelligence hacker and a master of disguise. Very little else is known about him other than he is a follower of the beliefs of the ancient oriental warrior general Sun Tzu. Almost everything he says is followed by a quote from one of Sun Tzu's many manuscripts. In the underworld, there is a $5 million bounty on his head for any information exposing the true identity of Cibermole. Without Cibermole we would not be able to identify and react effectively to exploits by the black hats until after they took place. We would not be able to understand how the organisation functioned and who does what. We would not be able to properly safeguard those who are the victims and we would not have the confidence to know that if this hacker cell were ever to be compromised that we'd cause untold damage to them before they took us down.

Spies like Cibermole

```
Your surviving spy must be a man of keen
    intellect, though in outward appearance
    a fool; of shabby exterior, but with a
    will of iron.

He must be active, robust, endowed with
    physical strength and courage:

Thoroughly accustomed to all sorts of dirty
    work, able to endure hunger and cold,
    and put up with shame and ignominy.

Sun Tzu (5th Century BC)
```

Jaqs [me] (the messenger)

Someday when the black hats have gained enough information on the people of the world, they will begin to close off parts of the Internet. They will make sure that only they have access to the central information systems. Only they have overall control of the information superhighway.

Until then they intend to continue on with the illusion that the Internet is open to everyone. What you will see is a continued programme to regulate communications, to find out who you are speaking to and to eavesdrop on what you were talking about. Their agenda is to pressure governments into passing laws that will ensure that everything you do is monitored and to reduce your liberty and your freedom of speech and movement. These people would go so far as to cause problems in the world in order to get what they want. To use the media to alienate those who could pose a real threat to their agenda. To use those who are weak as bait and to draw attention away from the real agenda.

When you turn on your TV can you really be sure that the information you're given is accurate? Do you really believe everything you hear without ever challenging it? Unfortunately, for most people the answer is yes, because they don't feel they have any real power to find the truth in any other way. By the age of 12 I could speak 3 languages other than English - Arabic, French and German. By 15 I was reading foreign websites and getting the news from all over the world and comparing what was being said. This has taught me that there is more than one side to any story. As the messenger in the team I have learnt to translate the subversive messages of the black hats and to design new tools and languages for communication that cannot be intruded upon. I have learnt that we must seek to reduce dependency on technology by gaining control of it and to build networks of trust between friends and citizens that cannot be subverted by the evil agenda of the black hats.

Would you like to to work as computer hacker? Could you be one? Could you be an engineer like Sykes or a navigator like Smouth, or a healer like Noah? Or maybe you'd like the excitement of being a spymaster like Cibermole or a Messenger like me? Maybe you've something else in mind?

Lean, Clean Communications
Hackers are lean, in body and in mind
They only touch text, the truth is in text
Images distort, too much illusion
Teletype devices are good
Communication needs clarity, no confusion
The world needs a different kind of beauty
The beauty of purity, goodness, honesty
Hackers are honest, they solve problems
They care not for cheap talk
They care only for honest expression
Honest expression must not be debased by aesthetic richness, graphics, images etc
Voice must be simple and basic
It must be drawn from those with pure in motive
Those who take responsibility for their actions
It must contain the facts,
It must reveal the meaning, the truth
When the white hat types... they express the truth with every strike of their hand. Only then can they be sure they are a truly operating in the spirit of the hacker. <u>Jamie</u>

Chapter 3 – Hacker World – by Jaqs

Droids

Every time you login to the Internet, the computer creates your very own cyber character. As you type on the keyboard this character changes and begins to move.

These expressions are known as droids and have high or low intelligence depending on the ability of the user it belongs to. As you develop your Internet skills your droid signature evolves and becomes more and more intelligent.

When you're in the zone, droids look like animated characters roaming through the Internet. Those that belong to novice users are usually more vaguely constructed and are therefore much easier to disrupt and destroy.

Droids that are well constructed and move at lightening speed belong to the professional users and have advanced onboard systems. The most advanced droids are those that belong to the hackers. Other advanced droids include those that are programmed by your computer system or by the people who maintain the Internet (administrators).

When you logon to the Internet your droid is activated immediately and the system then identifies you as its user. Most people never realise that their actions create these droids. It is only possible to actually see these droids, if your mind has truly entered the Zone.

Hackers that can think deeply about their time and behaviour on the Internet are best placed to make the greatest contribution to our cause. It is better to see your enemy and sense their movements by getting in the Zone, than only be able to see the computer screen in front of you. As you type, you should never simply see the software interface in front of you, you need to visualise how it is affecting the battle beyond.

You need to think in Cyber Characters. ----

In the Zone, we actually visualise the battles. We see all.

```
                                     .·Ya·.
       ·-·           ·····-·: ·:····.                    .·········
       ··                    ·:····:·· · ·····. ···      ·····:··
       ···                 .. ·····-······:YYVYY:YY········· . ···    ··.  ····.
       ···                  ·····-······.  ·:····.  ···:···YY········.··.  ·Y··.
       ···                  ··.·······.  ·:···. ············:············
       ···               ...······YYY·.   ··IYY         ······:·····YY·.     ·YY·.
       ···                     .···········-··· :·             ..··········.  .·Y·.
       ···                     .YY······-···· ···:.                ··········I.
       ···                   ·······:·····YY·.    ··· ·······.   ·······:·· ·········.
       ···                  ···YY·····:·YY·······......·· ···Y······. ·····:········
       ···                   ····················:·······.... ········· .············YIYYY
       ···                      ·········YYYY·..   ········YY·····.   ············YYYYYY
       ···                       ·······::···YY········. ········.   ·YYY········
       ···                       ·····YYYYYY···········.    ·YYYYYY
       ···              ·.     ··YYYY:················.  ·YYYYYY
       ···                    ·YYYY:··········YY·······.    ·YYYYYY
       ···               ··  ··YY·····YY··YY·······.     ·YYYYY··YY
       ···                    ·YYYYY:···YYYYY········.     ·YYYYY
       ···                    ·YYYY···YY·····:YYYYY·.        ·YYYYYY
       ···                    ·YYYYY·····YY:·······Y·         ·YYYYYY
       ···                    ·YYYYY········YYY····. ···. ·YYY··
       ···                    ·YYYY:YY···YYY:·······.   ·YYYY:·
       ···             ·YY·   ·YYYY:YY·YY···YY·Y···YYY.    ·YYYYY
       ···              ·Y·    ··YYYY:YY······ .YYY·YYY  ·YYYY·
       ···          ·YY  ·Y·  ···YYY·····ZZ·Y··YYYIYY·  ·····.
       ···         ·Y··YY·     ·YYY·· · ····Y··YY·······.   ·YYYYY·.
       ···         ·YYYY······   ·YYY·· · ······YYYYYY·. · YYYYYYY·.
       ···       ····YY··YYYY······ · ·.·  ·YYYYY··YYYYY··YYYYYY
       ···           ·YY······YYYYYY            ··YYY··YYYYYYYY·YYYY·····
       ···          ···YY·YYYYYYYYYY·:     ·YYYYY·YY·Y··YY·····YYYYY·····
       ···         ··YYY·YYY··.··    ·YYYYYY···YY.·····    ·YY·. ···YYY··.  ········
       ···         ·YYYYYY··YYY·.   ·YYYY·     ·YYYYY··YYYYY··.    ········
       ···           ·YY···YYYY··········:         ····Y·.               ···.
       ···    ·YY······YY·YY.. ·YYYYYY···YY·. ······YY·  ··  ···Y·····.    ········
       ···               ·YY·Y.    ·YYYY·         ·YY·.  ·YY··. ·······
       ···                ·YY·Y      ·YY·····    ·Y··.   ·YY······  ·YY
       ···                 ···  ···YY··   ·YY·:YYY··YYY··· ··  ·YY········
       ···                          ·Y·····          ·YY
       ···              ·YY···YY·YYY········             ··YY
       ···              ·YY········YY········   ··YYYYY···   ·YY·.
       ···            ·······YYYYYY···YYYY······    ·YY····.    ·YY
       ···     ·              ·YY·· ·YYYY················  ···.·YY·.
       ···     ·              ··YYYY· ·· ·YY·····YYY··YY·  ··YY·····
       ···     ·                ·YY·YY···········   ·YY·.
       ···     ·                 ·YY··  ·YYY·Y···YY···YY·.
       ···     ·                  ·YY·Y·  ·YY····· YY·YY·
       ···     ·                       .                                    ·YY
       ···     ·                 ·YY·······YY·:              ·YY·YY·Y·YY·YY·
       ···     ·                  ·Y·YY·:YYY ··· ··                         ·YY
       ···     ·                   ·YYYYY· :YY··  ·                      ·Y·YYY·····
       ···     ·                        ·                               ·Y·YYYY·.
       ···     ·                    ·YYYYY  ·YY· ··                  ·
       ···     ·                     ··  ·     ·
       ···     ·                        ·YYY· · ·Y ···
```

Image depicting a droid being attacked by black hat hackers when viewed from inside the zone. When seen from outside the zone, you only see messages and descriptions of the battle on your computer screen.

Programmers

You may have heard of a bunch of people called "Computer Programmers".

These people have an ability to construct computer programs. Computer programs are lists of instructions that make your computer do some kind of work.
For instance a computer program can make the letter you have typed up output the words to your printer or it can help you to send your holiday photos over the Internet to your friends, wherever they may live. Some computer programs check for viruses, some help you make websites, draw pictures and entertain you and so on.
Programmers also write programs that help you to search for things on the Internet and to protect your computer from intruders entering to steal and disrupt your files.

Programmers have an ability that far outweigh that of most ordinary users on the Internet. They have an ability to create the most powerful droids known to man because they can insert extra special computer codes whenever like. By simply adding in new instructions, they can alter the droid signature, to do anything they want to.

Computer users who are unable to write computer code are at a distinct disadvantage because they can only add a limited amount of power to their droids and these functions only usually work when the user is online.
Programmers can add extra powers to droids that work even when they themselves are fast asleep in bed. They can produce droids made out of code that never sleeps!
In short, users who are also programmers are able to build droids that operate 24 hours a day, 7 days a week, 365 days per year. For this reason most of the hacker fraternity is steeped in the art of computer programming.
Certainly everybody in Hacker Cell is.....

Learn how the Internet works first. Get proficient with it. Download tools and try new things out. Explore! Get your friends involved and enjoy your time online. Then when you feel ready to get more serious, begin to learn how to write computer programs and automate the things you like to do most online. Later, when you've mastered some of the art of programming, you'll be ready to take on new challenges. You'll be ready to turn your knowledge into hacking. White Hat hacking, I hope!

Get Coding, Get Hacking

```
IF BlackHat = "nearby"
{
      BlackHatName = Identifyhim();
      IF BlackHatName = "hackM"
      {
            output "it's a bad hacker";
            /* Run exploit on hackM; */
            RemoveHim(BlackHatName);
      }
            IF BlackHatStatus = "NOW DEAD"
            {
            output "Yippee";
            else
            Exit; /*get out of here*/
            }
      Exit
}
```

Users

There are three types of user on the Internet.

1. Novice and ordinary users:-
These are people who use the Internet for carrying out basic activities such as email or chat rooms, entertainment, searching for information that interests them or for promoting their businesses.

Super-User users:-
These are people who do everything that novice and ordinary users do, but also purchase computer programs that do much more sophisticated work, such as achieving high rankings in search engines or for scanning the Internet to find out which sites are advertising their products.

Elite Users:-
These are programmers and hackers who use their skills to add extra-special powers to their online activities. Amongst these users you will find all sorts of subversive types, from computer virus makers to trojan horse fiends to email bombers and the exclusive clubs that monitor the behavioural patterns of every participant on the Internet.
When you're in the Zone, how you see the world of the Internet will depend on what level of user you are.

Novice users can only see the obvious things, like what is on their computer screen at any one time. Whereas Elite users think mainly about what is going on beyond their computer screens. They need to be able to visualise the online behaviour of their opponents so they can make the right moves. This can only be achieved if they are concentrating more on the things that are going on under the hood and not on the obvious things.
Like how do you get this #$#* mouse to work?

Landscape

When you enter the ZONE, it isn't just the visitors and operatives that look familiar, because the actual online world seems to resemble everything we see in the real world.

You see, the Internet is merely a mirror image of the real world. Made in the image of man, a space where man can escape from the earthly limitations of real world. A place where they can still feel at home, even if the surroundings are imaginary. A place where we can communicate with our friends on the other side of the world, at a flick of a switch. A place where we can take action in the privacy of our own homes.

On the Internet, there are many of the same structures and objects that we enjoy in real world. There are highways for transportation, banks and shopping malls, businesses and art galleries. There are schools and libraries and entertainment centres of every kind.

On the Internet, you can create your very own poster homepage and invite anyone in the world along to tell them everything about you. There are communities of every kind, from people with interests in sports to special groups debating important issues, news, politics and religion etc.

When you are an elite user and you are in the Zone you see everything. You see the highways, the buildings, the forests and the trees. You see the communities and you see the millions of droids that tread the landscape each day.
Outside the Zone, the only thing you see is the interface of the computer software and the computer you loaded it on. Inside we see everything. Outside we see everything.

Why don't you join us and see it all to?

Movement

Everything moves fast on the Internet. Droids come and go. One second another droid is online talking to your droid, the next second they've been disconnected by their user and they hang-up and disappear. Sometimes never to be seen again.

When you type instructions into your computer your droid begins to move and carry out the tasks you had instructed it to do. Whether it is a request to connect to a website or an instruction to send an email to a friend, it matters not. Your droid is working hard to service your every command.

When you scan and remove viruses from your computer, your droid is actually doing battle with the many other droids that the black hats have sent to invade your personal computer space. When you speak on the Internet, your droid is actually transporting messages between you and the person communicating with you.

The Internet is a cylindrical type structure which is not surprising given the Internet is made up of zillions of wires connected together by billions of computers. Each wire is only so big. Some wires are massive and can carry billions of droids all travelling fast to their destination at the same time. However, many wires can only fit a limited amount of traffic at the same and can easily become congested when too many droids are travelling at once.

Congestion is a particularly bad problem where droids are tasked with carrying large image files as an attachment to say an email. Sometimes the reason why the Internet can appears to go slow.

If you use broadband, cable or something similar you will find that droids will work more quickly with your instructions because the pipeline is wider than that of a dial-up telephone line using an old fashioned computer modem.

Other Worlds

There are literally millions of worlds connected to the Internet. Your kettle is a piece of technology that can today be instructed by you at your computer keyboard. Your garage door, your washing machine, the electronics in your car.... even that old electric powered chair that your Granny uses to get around. Wicked!!!!

Today everything is becoming wired and that means that instructions that work in one world can now be used in a completely different world. It also means that there is even more landscape to patrol and to defend from the evil doers.

--_SCAN Computer Gateway

WELCOME to COMPUTER Gateway <press enter>

Hi...greetings from Chris's bedroom network_____

--_LIST OBJECTS PRESENT

1. Coffee Maker Present
2. MP3 Files Present
3. Interesting Pictures of Girlfriend Present
4. Stolen School Exams Present
5. Photo of my Mum on the Toilet Present

Please select an option to gain access....

Security

Like the real world, the Internet is inherently insecure. Like the real world, there are border controls where you are asked for your passport to cross over to the other side. Like the real world, there are security measures in place to prevent criminals from damaging and stealing goods and information. Like the real world there are people policing the Internet to try and keep you safe all year round.

But unlike the real world most of the online world is accessible to anyone at a click of a button. Unlike real world, if you wanted to steal something from Brazil you could do it without ever going there. You can disrupt and subvert large organisations without even stepping foot in the door. Without even knowing what they do, what they stand for. Effectively meaning that it is impossible to stop all criminal behaviour on the Internet. There are just too many entry points and just too many different ways of breaking in, pilfering and covering your tracks.

At best, all most people can do is install the latest security programs and make sure they don't upset the wrong people.

Fall out with a black hat and you could find yourself subjected to many years of abuse, with no good way of stopping it from happening.

Unless you change your identity completely of course!
But that is pretty radical stuff indeed.

AND IT RARELY SOLVES THE PROBLEM ANYWAY.

Intrenchment

Have you ever been held so tight that you couldn't move? That you couldn't breathe? Have you ever had one of those dreams where you were inside something and you couldn't get out? Where someone or something had you cornered and there was just no escape?
Well this is the feeling of Intrenchment.

When the hackers do battle inside the Internet what they seek to do is to freeze each other out of game.
To Intrench the target. To fix firmly and securely the enemy so they are incapable of fighting back. To reduce the movement of the other hacker, by freezing their droid out the game.

Only master hackers know the laws of Intrenchment, the underlying strategies that are used to intrench a target.

When a master hacker does battle with a lesser hacker you can be sure that it will result in the capture of the lesser hackers droid and their ultimate removal from the game.

AMBUSH THE BAD BEASTS

SURROUND THEM

QUARANTEEN THEM

CONTAIN THESE MONSTERS

ENTOMB THESE PREDATORS

FOR INTRENCHED THEY WILL SURELY LEAVE THIS PLACE

OR AT THE VERY LEAST HAVE NO IMPACT AT ALL

Zone~less~ness

You know when you've been in the Zone, when you've been typing at your keyboard and you suddenly become conscious that you've been sat in the same position for over 10 hours. When you're still drinking that same old coffee in the evening that you prepared in the morning. When you don't know the meaning of taking a break and bedtime is when you finally feel satisfied with the work you have done - which is usually sometime after 2am in the morning.

People say that hackers are negative, introvert, nerdy type people, when in actual fact the truth is that these opinions usually come from people with only half a brain. Trying to get us to think about them, rather than letting us concentrate on being in the Zone. Ok, it does look a little odd when you're trying to communicate with a zombie that seems to be ignoring you...

But the answer is ... to SHUTUP and GO AWAY!

When you are stuck half way between real world and the Internet, it can have a serious effect on you. What you have effectively done is to open yourself up to live and think in two worlds simultaneously and both are having an effect on you. You have offered yourself up to operate in two worlds so that you might play a more intelligent role.

So what if the bed isn't made! So what! Can't you see that I'm stuck between two worlds, right now!

If you cannot find your way into the ZONE, then you will have to remain on the fringes of the new world. Unfortunately for you, this will mean that you will always remain an outsider. Someone with a blurred vision of the world. Someone who has limited control of your identity. Lack of power over the things that frighten you on the Internet.

You will never truly know what is going on under the hood of your computer. You just won't get it!!! And that puts you RIGHT IN THE FIRING LINE OF THE BLACK HATS.

ZONELESS – NESS (on the diskette)

BEWARE OF REMAINING OUTSIDE THE ZONE

FOR YOU SHALL BE KNOWN AS AN IGNORANT ONE

ONE OF THOSE BACKWARD TYPES THAT CANNOT MAKE THE TRANSITION FROM 20TH TO 21ST CENTURY.

ONE OF THOSE WHO CANNOT CONJURE THE DISCIPLINE AND MOTIVATION TO JOIN THE BATTLE AGAINST FEAR AND OPPRESSION.

MY ADVICE TO YOU IS TO GET IN THE ZONE.

AND MAKE SURE YOU STAY THERE FOR ALL TIME. LEST YOU FIND YOURSELF AMONGST THE VICTIMS, THE DEFENSLESS, THE DOMINATED KIND.

Chapter 4 – Hacker Behaviour – by Smouth

Composers

Hackers are like composers and musicians all rolled into one. They compose the hack and then they play it out on their keyboards - sometimes at lightening speed. When they clash with a black hat, the symphony they play can produce millions of lines of code and the performance can be played out over many days. The resulting display can look extremely dramatic. The players are the black and the white hat droids created by hacker hands typing on the keyboard. Put your mind in the zone, place your hands on the keyboard, activate the command line and commence battle!

Of course the best hackers are more likely to spend the majority of their time in the backroom building tools than necessarily in the frontline wrestling with the bad guys all day. When elite hackers strike they strike quickly and unleash sophisticated computer code packages to do the fighting for them.

You don't get a dog and bark right, so why would you spend hours in a battle when you can build a tool and deploy it against the target and get it to do the fighting for you? This is a much more convenient and smarter way of hacking because once the tools are designed you can use them anywhere and at anytime. So say you don't want your computer to be traced while you are working at the command line – wouldn't it be better to go online, install a tool on a another computer, activate the program and then disconnect from the Internet whilst it launches its attack on the black hat target. You can then go back online later and check out what occurred during the battle.

This way you get to carry out the exploit and avoid detection from the black hat you are targeting.

Whether you design sophisticated toolkits to do your fighting for you or you do battle interactively matters not, the common way of the hacker is to use the command line.

You can play at hacking using graphical user interfaces (GUI's), but you cannot enter the Zone unless you use the command line.
When you switch on to a command line, you can feel it drawing you closer, drawing you farther and farther into the Zone. You feel its power. You want to be part of it. You want to express that inner piece of your soul through it. To project it inside the Internet and to make it touch other peoples souls.

Command Line gives hackers the freedom they need to do their work. To crawl through and around into spaces that other interfaces could never take you. To develop tools that can be deployed against a target quickly and that leave no trace. To give you the confidence that you can defend your own computer from attack because the Command Line gives the ability to see everything that is going on under the hood. Command Line empowers you to learn the things that the black hats don't want you to learn.

Command Line gives you power to take control of your life. To fight against those that unchallenged would undermine humanity. To lead you towards learning the true ways of the hacker.
To take INDEPENDENCE, so you control technology – not it you.

If you decide to become a white hat in the future, don't spend too much money.
You just need a Command Line and an Internet connection.
The cheapest computer will do!
TO ENTER THE ZONE – USE A COMMAND LINE ONLY.

Engagers

As I touch the keys the movement of my hands and the code on the screen become synchronised. As the battle reaches its climax, my mind and body seem to transcend all worlds and I find myself in a different space entirely. Face to face with my evil adversary. Everything slows down in this space, yet the typing on the keyboard is speeding up.

This black hat is a VirusNerd type. Its user is Stelfoss, a black hat virus kit builder, based in Berlin, Germany.
Its been a long time since I did battle with a VirusNerd, the last time was 2001 when NomScoy - again out of the StelFoss stable took half of the UK banking systems out for over 2 hours. I've seen this type before, its been a long time but I still remember its attack signature. I still remember its counter-offensive strategies. This shouldn't take long, I understand its posture. How could I not -

It's RIGHT IN FRONT OF ME
Now it's seen me, it has started to replicate itself. YUK, there are 2 now and 4 and 8 and 640!!!! Better move fast. It's getting crowded in here.

Ok how to handle this situation? Ok, let's use the original "NomScoy Killer script"

Change the name of the file to "Tartus Killer Tool [TKT] !" (the name of this particular dead beat) and………..

--_ DEPLOY [TKT] to DROIDS LIKE "TARTUS DROID" Finished?

--_ LIST ALL COMBAT DROIDS PRESENT
➢1. JAQS Present

DONE, bye bye Tartus DROID.

GOING DEEPER INTO THE ZONE

THERE IS A PREDATOR AND IT IS NOT ME

BUT I CERTAINLY DO KNOW IT

COZ I SEE EVERYTHING IT CAN SEE

WHEN I ENTER THE ZONE

AND IT ENTERS ME

I CAN BE AND DO LIKE ANYTHING OR ANYONE I SEE

FOR THIS IS THE PLACE WHERE I CAN BE ANY IDENTITY

FROM BLACK HAT TO WHITE HAT

I CAN CHOOSE TO BE ANYTHING I SEE

THE BEASTS THINK THE ZONE IS FOR THEM TO TAKE ME

BUT WHEN I ARRIVE WHAT DO THEY SEE

SOMETHING THAT IS AS POWERFUL AS THEY CAN BE

SOMETHING THAT IS EVERY BIT AS FREE

HERE TO WIPE AWAY THE DARKNESS AND TO DEFEND HUMANITY

Enablers

I can see you bad beasts. I can be you bad beasts. I see what you see bad beasts. I can be as you bad beasts. What your motives are, what your plans are, how you desire to take us down. What it is you want, the power you lust over.

In the Zone I will take you down. Inhabit you and pull you apart before your very eyes. Think not that black hats are all powerful. Think not that only bad beasts can play these games. For the white hats will do anything to remove you from the game. For the white hats are not talkers of action or bystanders. We will do anything to take you out - to take you down. Anything!

Beware bad beasts that when you enter the Zone that you do not find us present. For we will sense you out and then you will be history.

We are the enablers of the Internet generation. You are the disablers, the wreckers – the backward types.

We fear not, for we know that what we are and do is the only thing worth living for. When we are not here we will stop and our brothers and sisters will fight on.
In our minds there is no pain, there is only justice. Only freedom, only peace.

So let us in black hats and we will turn your minds away from evil and selfishness and towards the light.
Let us in and we will enable you to see the error of your ways and that what you fight for is a flawed cause.
Let us in, don't resist us and you will surely be saved.
So that when you come to the end of your life and prepare to meet your maker, your conscience will be clear and you will lay in everlasting peace.

Exploiters

"Resist and you shall suffer the cuts of 100 hundred thousand white hat droids". Resist and you shall be intrenched. Entombed inside your bad behaviour for ever more. Never to return to the free days when you roamed the Internet savaging and maiming everything in your path.
Exploit is always the last resort for us.

In Exploit our perspective changes. When we switch to Exploit Mode, there are no emotions. There is no fear. There is no second thoughts. There is just the plan. When we choose a target for Exploit, we create our plan of attack. Then we put it into action.

Our plan always includes five stages:
1. Assess the layout of the Battleground
2. Profile the Opponents
3. Design Attack Plan
4. Activate Defense Strategy
5. Initiate Attack!

When we attack we visualise the battleground. We know our objectives and we see the profile of opponents in front us. We mount the attack and put the defense strategy into operation.

We do this united as a group and resolved in our beliefs, each one of us committed to working for a common cause. Each one of us contributing something special. Each one of us watching each others back. It is said that the whole is greater or equal to the sum of all parts. This is true of our group.
This is true of all white hat cells. This is true because cells contain hackers that are chosen to compliment each other. Counter-Terrorism Assault Groups such as ours always comprise an engineer, a healer, a messenger, a navigator and a leader and super agent, like Cibermole.

Intrenchers

When the battle is over, when we have defeated the enemy - then it will be intrenched. Its droid signature will have been identified and we will have applied the antidote. It will never again be able to wreak so much havoc. Never again take so many by surprise, for it will be known and we will be ready next time we sense its signature. Next time it will be removed from the game as soon as it is released on to the Internet.
Yet the droid is merely a slave in the employ of its user!

Slaying the droid is not the same as slaying the user. For we know that all the time the human user is free, it is unlikely we will have seen the last of its treacherous ways. Maybe next time it will seek revenge by unleashing a droid monster so great that it will take half of the Internet out for a day.
Maybe next time it will want to make doubly sure that it cannot be beaten. Maybe next time it will try to infiltrate our group and take us from inside. Maybe next time it will bring all its buddies along for the fight.

To remove the scourge we must remove the black hat user that creates and controls the droids. We must find ways of removing the puppet master, not just the simple puppet. For it is the human beast we seek to intrench, not simply the droid actions it creates. Until it is torn away from its computer, there will be more evil droids. More cunning ways. More cruelty and malice. More sinister agendas and more fear and anxiety of our kind.
Our masters understood the power of Intrenchment. They taught us to understand how it should be used and who and what it is best targeted at.

Beware Devil Black Hats!
We are watching you. We are watching for your behaviour.

Chapter 5 – Predatory Minds –by Cibermole

There are those who believe that the black hats are from a distant planet. There are those who believe that they are from a race of monsters, similar to the raptors in the blockbuster movie Jurassic Park. But the simple fact is that none of these beliefs are true. The simple fact is that the black hats are people like you and me. They are human beings and they are different only by the flawed beliefs that they hold.

Their actions are simply a result of holding the beliefs they do. They have chosen to follow the deadly sins, the selfish, rather than choose to follow the path that leads toward GOOD.

They think and behave like the predators in Jurassic Park, but they do not take the form of these lizards - which if you think about it is an even worse nightmare, given it is much more difficult to track them down and expose them.

Have you ever followed someone home in the dark?
Do you feel their fear? Do they keep looking back? Can you sense their anguish as you draw closer? Never knowing whether you might take them from behind. Pulling them to the floor. Devouring them piece by piece as their screams go unheard. Understand that this is the condition of the predatory mind. Can you feel the power of the predator?
Can you feel the power of the dark side? Its attraction is strong and there are many who have crossed over, never to find their way back again.
In the days when man had to hunt to feed his family these predatory instincts were vital to his survival.
Today the predatory mind is used to covet other people's possessions, to subvert good causes and to spread the influence of the devil to the far corners of the earth.

SEEK IT NOT, FOR IT WILL SEEK YOU – BEWARE!!!

Do you recognise the power of the predatory mind? Have you seen it before? Either in yourself or the actions of others? Would the world be a better place full of predators, or would it be a better place without predators? Without those who pretend that humanity is somehow in need of such flawed attributes?

Black Hat Chant (on diskette)

There are those who do not know

They do not know they are being watched

They do not know what they do is not of their making

Who believe that they are free and that the actions they take are done from their own hands. Their own minds. Their own hearts.

They do not know that we make them do the things they do.

They do not know that we can do this at any time.

For their hearts, minds and souls are ours.

Ours. Ours for all time.

Ours to take as we want.

Dark Strategies

Never simply watch the actions of any one thing and think that there is nothing else to see. Try to see beyond the obvious. Look for the causes, the behaviour patterns and the motives behind any particular event. When a problem occurs, never listen to only one point of view. Listen to many and then form your opinion. Never act before understanding why you should do so. Clarify every issue, master every act. Concentrate on the task in hand.

These words are etched in the experience of many battles with the black hats. For they are masters in the art of deception. Masters in the application of illusory devices, seeking to influence through lies and trickery. To elevate their own position at the expense of others.

Always protecting their own kind.

Black hat strategies are many, but none are so potent as the art of indirection. What the eye cannot see the mind does not understand. This is the formula that lies at the heart of their evil agenda. The types of problems they like us to think about are:-

How can I give this thing to you, that you don't need, in such a way that you won't remember where you got it from?

or

How can I give this thing to you, that you do need, in such a way that you never truly own it – but you believe you do?

The Art of Indirection is a way of thinking that has to be mastered over a long period of time but once you attune your mind to it you gradually begin to think the way that black hats do. You gradually begin to approach life differently. Always looking for the angles first. Looking for ways to fiddle with peoples thoughts without them realising. Ways of manipulating the subconscious mind rather than interacting on a conscious, natural level. Do you think these guys are smart? Well think again! They are just selfish, devious-minded criminals without a conscience.

Watch the picture below. Can you see the scene? What does this picture tell you? Would you know what to do? Is this a typical problem with car-parks? Something that we all have to put up with? Or is this a BLACK HAT TRAP, using the ART OF INDIRECTION to trick us into stealing our money??

```
Pay $1 if you park in the left hand bay
before 9am, but pay $2 in the right hand
bay after 6pm. But if you park in either
after 9am - then it is free.
But not today.
Immediate $50 fine, if you park
incorrectly!
```

Deadly Posture

One of the most important questions is - how can you tell a black hat from any one else? How is it possible to identify black hat activity?

It is true that each and everyone of us has the ability to do both GOOD and EVIL, so quite often you might identify someone as a black hat only to find that their deeds turn into something good. Most people are stuck half way between black hat and white hat territory. They are "either-or", which is extremely confusing for them. One day they can play life dirty, the next day they turn into saints. This is the way most human beings behave. Nobody is perfect right?

To become a black hat or white hat it is necessary to swear allegiance and to follow a path toward becoming one or the other. Given the secrecy surrounding the black hats it is unlikely that you would ever be able to tell who they were. Unless you were a trained white hat of course!

White hats receive the training that is essential to being able to engage black hat targets and to infiltrate them to confirm that they are who they say they are.

There are many ways of identifying the type of hat you are dealing with, the majority of which involves probing and testing the target, checking the results of the tests and then improving the level of testing, until you begin to build a pattern of the type of character you are dealing with. It is important not just to look at your test results but to also assess the behaviour of the target during testing. Most people fall into three different categories....

White Hat, Black Hat or OC's for Ordinary Citizens.

What you're looking for from the testing is to ascertain the true posture of the target. People are not always what they seem to be! What they appear to be and the posture they maintain is quite often FALSE.

There are people who walk around saying how great they are when in actual fact, deep down, these people believe they are pretty useless. But they spend their lives saying how brilliant they are in order to cover up for a real lack of confidence in themselves.

White hats know the benefits of working on the light side. They know that they never have to be false. Never have to hide who they really are. Never have to feel bad about who they are and conceal their motives. They know that they can speak and do freely and that what they say is natural and meant with the best intentions.

You know automatically when there are black hats around when the OC's are behaving like sheep, or when they are frightened out of their wits by certain people being around. This is a good way to locate a source. Look at the behaviour of groups of ordinary citizens. Then by further analysis of key people you can begin to get an idea which people to target using more in-depth investigations.

You never round these people up and begin to work on them. You always target them individually and work on them for a while. Condition them accordingly and then if necessary put them in the same space together and see how they perform.

Watch their behaviour, see how they respond. Do they have anything to hide? Are there a number of black hats collaborating together here? How can you tell from their behaviour which ones are the black hats? Are some using indirection to hide and redirect attention? Why are they trying to hide? Are they black hats or are they OC's with a confidence problem? JOIN THE WHITE HATS AND LEARN HOW TO TELL!

Chapter 6 – Hacker Training – *by Noah*

Body Training

Think you don't need a physical body to become a hacker? Think it doesn't matter if your body is out of shape, as long as your fingers still move? Well, you're wrong! Whether you are able bodied or disabled, matters not. If you want to become an elite hacker then you need to make your body fit. We are all made up of vibrational fields. If you are super fit then your vibrational field aligns more closely with nature and this reduces anxiety and gives you more capacity to operate effectively as a Hacker.

It's as simple as that. Unfortunately we never get to see a before and after picture to convince ourselves that body training is absolutely essential to operating as an elite hacker. You don't see how well you performed when you had a body looking like a giant potato versus when you had trained your body into a lean, mean, fighting machine.

Don't get me wrong, we're not talking about what your body looks like here, we're talking about the kind of mindset that you are going to need to become an elite hacker. You need to be able to understand that you need to train your body. To allow your mind to become the master of your body. Not the other way around.

It doesn't matter what you do to increase your fitness, as long as you do it. Your brain controls your central nervous system and every organ in your body. If you don't train your body then it becomes more difficult for your brain to control these systems and puts extra load on your brain. Which in turn means that your brain has less capacity to support your hacking.

So train your body. Train it with eating the right foods, drinking plenty of water. Train it with sleeping 7-8 hours per day. Train it with the right physical exercise. Train it with the right breathing and relaxation. Train it for stamina, for strength and for speed and agility. Train your body and it will be grounded in the real world and will set your hacker mind free.

BODY TRAINING (on the diskette)

BODY MUST BE FIT

IT MUST EAT WELL

IT MUST SLEEP WELL

IT MUST RUN WELL

THIS WILL INCREASE THE RESOURCES AVAILABLE FOR THE MIND

BODY FITNESS WILL ENABLE THE MIND TO COMMUNICATE WITH OTHERS BETTER

IT WILL ENABLE THE MIND TO STORE INFORMATION BETTER AND TO PROCESS IT BETTER

IT WILL ENABLE THE MIND TO BECOME BETTER ORGANISED AND THIS REDUCES FEAR AND ANXIETY LEAVING GREATER CAPACITY FOR CREATIVITY

THE BODY MUST BE TRAINED BECAUSE IT IS THE ENGINE ROOM

TRAIN THE ENGINE ROOM AND YOU WILL HAVE FAR GREATER CAPACITY TO DEAL WITH LIFE

BODY TRAINING IS THE BASIS FOR DEVELOPING THE MIND OF AN ELITE HACKER.

IN TIME THE NOVICE HACKER WILL TURN TO LEARNING THE WAYS OF PHYSICAL COMBAT BUT THIS WILL BE FOR SOMETIME AFTER THEY HAVE GAINED THIS ELEMENTARY MASTERY OVER THE BODY.

MAKE A BODY TRAINING PLAN AND STICK TO IT!

Behaviour Training

Hackers are different from ordinary citizens (OC's), so if you are intending to become a white hat, don't expect to behave like an OC. You will find that many of your friends and family will ridicule you for being different, but this is all part of the life of n hacker. But if you can't take this criticism then you won't make it as a white hat.

You need to know that it is ok to be different. It is ok, because what you do, the causes you fight for, are likely to change your behaviour. You will find that you start to realise that your time is more precious than ever before. That it is essential that you use your time wisely and not fritter it away in idle pursuits. Don't get me wrong, you don't stop having fun and taking part in other interests. You just get your kicks from combat in the Internet zone and from the buzz of saving thousands of people from distress and inconvenience.

As you train toward becoming an hacker you will begin to learn the value of words like LEAN, INDEPENDENT, TRUST, PREDATOR and INTRENCH (LITPI). These five words form the core of the belief system upon which our behaviour is based.

LEAN'ness is how we think, how we live and how we act. Everything we say and do is done with the utmost LEAN. This is to say that we never waste anything, neither time nor energy. We use it absolutely wisely. We never use anything or anybody unless we can see right through them. We are in complete control of our minds and bodies. We are in complete control of our art. We are the LEAN MACHINE.

INDEPENDENCE is what we seek above all. We operate independently, but we also work as part of a team. But if tomorrow there were no team, then we could each carry on independently. Very few people today are truly independent.

Very few can honestly say that they ever had a truly independent thought. One that wasn't placed there by some black hat or other stronger force. Very few can say that if there were no other people in the world tomorrow that they would still be able to survive. Very few would have an ability to work and live a life independent from anyone or anything else.
Elite hackers learn to operate totally independently. They learn to survive the things that most would turn away from. They learn the value of independence. Of being in control of their fears and being able to fend for themselves and others in times of great strife.
To become a hacker you need to learn the path toward INDEPENDENCE and too stay on it.
Honesty and integrity are the lifeblood of humanity.
From these two principles spring communities of healthy relationships, established from strong bonds of TRUST.
As a White Hat you will learn that your mission is to ensure that TRUST is maintained at the highest level on Internet. For the level of trust is the truest indicator of who is winning the battle for the Internet. So as a white hat you will learn to monitor the levels of trust on the Net and take action where TRUST is being undermined by Black Hats.
To become a hacker you need to understand that you are not your body and you are not your mind. You are that which uses your body and mind. You need to realise that you need to control your body and mind and use them to get what you want. You need to fine tune these vehicles and become a PREDATOR yourself. A hunter, a targeter of evil actions.
As you develop you will understand the minds and behaviours of the ugly demons & sharpen your mind in order to INTRENCH their ways effectively. You will learn how you can become them and still fight them and you will learn how to concentrate your mind so intensely that you can see right through their agenda and into the heart of the beast.
Maybe someday, you will join an elite hacker cell and become like the hydra hacker.

Learning Training

Hackers are ferocious learners, but we don't just learn for the sake of it, we learn what we need, when we need to.

We are dedicated to our craft and we study the ways and methods and materials that lead to greater mastery of hacking with the purpose of defeating the black hats. We never overload our mind, we keep it clear of too much knowledge. Free from the heaviness of information that we don't need. Hacker minds are like fine tuned instruments, ready to scan the next target and to out-think the enemy in battle. Probably the greatest attribute of any hacker is their unstinting ability to concentrate on becoming a better hacker. They block everything else out and only ever identify with playing the role of a hacker. They absorb hacking through their skin, they are like actors and great performers, and they never forget what their mission is.

To become a top hacker you need to train at least 12 hours per day. You need to commit your fingers to the keyboard for at least 10 hours of this time and live, sleep eat and breathe the life of an hacker. Every morning you get up and look in the mirror, you see a hacker. Every night you go to bed, you sleep like a hacker. Everything you say, wear and do is done like a hacker. Your personality is the personality of a hacker. To be the best in any area of life – you need to be seriously committed. You need to seriously believe in the cause you follow. Such is the style of the hacker. Such is the style of a winner.

So you need to begin with a commitment that learning the ways of the hacker is what you want and then stick with it. You need to prepare, like you have never prepared before.

You need to give your heart and soul to becoming a hacker. To give up the old ways and views of the ordinary citizen & to take hold of your life and do something really worthwhile with it. To do this you must first learn how to learn.

Great hackers are made not born, for we all have it in us to achieve greatness in this respect. As the tree cannot blossom without roots, trunk, branches and leaves, so too cannot the expertise of a hacker without the right foundations in place.

Without roots, trunk, branches and leaves, how can it be possible to enlarge the tree? Our masters have taught us that we should not learn one single thing, unless we are sure why we are learning it and for what purpose it serves. There can be no benefit to knowledge unless it is going to be useful. Unless there is a purpose to knowledge, what use is it? Unless it can save lives or feed the world's children, remove threats or increase opportunity – what use is it? Save fuelling someone's ego from time to time or plotting to use this knowledge in some evil way.

As the students mind and body is trained it has to take up the study of structured learning. This learning is how you develop the MIND of an hacker. What behaviour, what knowledge, what methods, what tools, what causes, and what threats.

This foundation of learning is called

The WAY OF THE TREE'

First you will establish the roots of your knowledge, then the trunk, then some branches and some leaves. This learning method will equip you with all you need to go out into the world and increase your hacker know-how, so that you can add more branches and leaves in the future.

The teachings of the Way Of The Tree are an exercise in developing your mental and physical tools to such a level that at the end of the exercise you will be able to operate effectively enough to join a hacker cell and to put your knowledge to good use. If you decide not to take on the challenge of becoming a hacker then Way of the TREE can be used to teach any other subject you care to follow.

Intelligence Training

There are many who use the term hacker to imply MENACE. These people do not seek to differentiate the meaning of "white hat" from "black hat". They seek to distort the meaning of terms.
To place all hackers in the same category.

Contrary to popular belief, white hats have less to do with computer security and more to do with national defence, intelligence and counter-terrorism. Sure we're involved in computer security, but we cover a much broader area than building security tools and applying hacker techniques.

Many of the problems with understanding what a white hat hacker does comes from the fact that most people don't understand how intelligence people work. Further confusion is caused because of out-dated definitions of the term white hat or by ill-conceived views from people in the computer security industry.
Some people think that white hats are simply people who explore computer systems for the purpose of locating security flaws so they can alert the software vendor and ordinary users. Others think of white hats as hobbyists who enjoy playing around with technology. Others think that they are ex-criminal hackers who have seen the error of their ways and now seek to make good by helping the authorities.
Well let me tell you that none of these descriptions are true.
White Hat hackers are intelligence people who give up their time to protect humanity from evil perpetrators.
They are experts in developing computer tools to automate their work. Masters in the art of surveillance and intelligence acquisition. Active in covert operations, linguistics and counter-terrorism. They are people who specialise in areas such as engineering, navigation, healing, communications, spying and the corruption of black hats.

When you enter the Zone you need more than a healthy interest in computer science to stay ahead of the game.
You need an imagination that puts you in the category of a trained intelligence officer.

Students must learn the tools and methods of the intelligence analyst. They must learn the nature of threats and targets. They must learn how to think like a skilled observer.
To identify and acquire knowledge and then to build models of battle scenarios in their heads. These scenarios they then use to assess where the vulnerability in question lies, what form of threat might be perpetrated, what the level of impact might be and how to mitigate the risk.
Intelligence hackers must be able to assimilate this information quickly and build an accurate model in their heads from which they can make decisions and take action.

Today's white hat hacker is no longer a long haired, whispy bearded, security geek. Today's white hat is a security professional with expert intelligence skills. Someone who cares about protecting the weak and vulnerable from the evil and predatory. Someone who is a highly trained individual and who uses their mind and fingers to do battle with the criminally unethical.

As the world becomes greatly more intrenched in the Internet it is essential that world governments train students of intelligence up to "white hat" level.
There can be no excuse for not training their agents to utilise the hands-on skills of the hacker.

There can be no excuse for not empowering AGENTS to use both the MINDS and HANDS of the White Hat hacker on the Internet.

Battle Training

Sun Tzu said, "it is one thing to be defeated, but quite another to have been surprised". It is also said that you should never enter a battle unless you are pretty certain you can win.

What these sayings mean is that you always need to be prepared for battle. To understand your enemy, the terrain and the causes for which they fight. To understand the troops and resources they have at their disposal and the reputation of their greatest warriors. You need to understand all these things and to assess your own strengths, weaknesses and strategies against those of your opponent, before you even think about doing battle with them.

Once you understand these things you should then be in a position to draw up a battle plan – OR NOT.
There is no disgrace in not engaging with the enemy until such time that you are sure you will win.

As a student you must learn the architecture of the battlefield and the strategies that will send you victorious. You must learn how to identify and to weigh the powers the enemy has at its disposal. To calculate the terrain and the order and structure of attack. To understand the motivation and level of resolve of the enemy troops and to work out where they might have weak points you can exploit. To determine your own weak points and to ensure a satisfactory defence and contingency plan.

In order to destroy the power of the beast you must seek to strike at its head, for this will disrupt its central nervous system, sending the rest of its body into a downward spiral.

Why walk through the battlefield, when you have the means to fly? THINK SMART, FIGHT SMART!

Battleground

zone → discover terrain

Class: Commercial, Military, Internet
Domain: Restricted, Unrestricted
Application: Human, System, Environmental

zone → discover assets
Software program-1, Software program-2

zone → discover vulnerability = Software program-1
<Alert! Prone to buffer overflow>

zone → discover threats
Virus_Nerd_Droid_Larsson in-the-room

zone → discover counter-measures
White_Hat_Smouth in-the-room

→ **Alert! Software program-1 is down!!!!!**

zone → discover Virus_Nerd_Droid_Larsson
Virus_Nerd_Droid_Larsson is IP 198.198.196.190

zone → deploy White_Hat_Smouth to IP 198.198.196.190
activate White_Hat_Smouth
<Virus_Nerd_Droid_Larsson has left-the-room!!!>

← *Recommend patching Software program-1* →

Cause Training

Fear not if you truly believe in what you fight for, for you will have the will to enter 1,000 battles without concern for your own limitations. Never do anything in life unless you truly believe in what you do. Never enter into any relationship nor set anyone's expectations above where they should be. For you must be honest with yourself as well as with others. Never do anything in life without the right intentions. Follow only worthy and honourable causes.

You will never hear such words from the black hats, because they spend most of their time concentrating on disrupting everyone else's causes, rather than sharing the joys of life with the rest of us.

They are so entrenched in their own lies and deceit that they actually believe they are fighting for a cause. When in actual fact, they are simply people programmed to break things. Programmed to misbehave in the worst kinds of ways. Imagine spending your life breaking things, rather than building things? Rather than helping people out of suffering. Rather than helping to educate and to protect.

What must it be like for those who only know how to subvert, corrupt and destroy? How would you feel when you meet your maker and they ask you what you've shared with your fellow creatures and you have to say:

"Well I've shared nothing my lord. In fact I've spent my whole life smashing souls and ensuring their downfall"
"But it was all for a worthy cause, honest!"

There is no training in causes for becoming a white hat hacker. You either get it or you don't.
If you have to think hard about following good causes, then I'd seriously advise you to consider a different profession.

You will have heard of the term "ENLIGHTENMENT".
This term typically means that you have reached a state of mind where you can see things differently. In fact you will be able to view the world in a much better way. In a way that helps you to live your life in better ways.

Our masters have all reached this enlightenment.
They believe that every human being on this planet is an artist. They believe that art isn't something produced like music, paintings or drama. They believe that art lies not in the artefact, but in the degree to which the expression of art is valuable to humanity.

How so much an artist is a painter who brings joy to a select few than the white hat hacker who through their action delivers millions out of spiritual slavery?

Ask not!

What is art?

Ask!

How significant is this art to mankind?

Join the white hats and you will reach enlightenment.

Join us in the Zone and fight for a cause that really means something.

Join us in the Zone – and unleash the ways of the white hat.

Chapter 7 – Hacker Techniques – *by Jaqs*

Covert Operations

We do much more than launch counter-hack offensives on black hats. We actually mount special operations using our own in-house designed guerrilla warfare system.

These techniques have been perfected over many years and we have mounted hundreds of covert operations against targets of every kind.

There is always a source (that's us) and there is always a target (that's a black hat). Quite often there are intermediaries involved, people who either provide us with vital information or who carry out some task on our behalf. We never operate from a specific brief. Our brief is to simply rid mankind of those who exhibit evil predatory behaviours.

This cause is our master – we serve nobody else save this cause. We never expect anyone outside of our group to be responsible for anything that they do not wish to be.

Sometimes there are multiple targets and sometimes there is a need to collaborate with other white hat groups around the world, in order to take the enemy down. Even though we are only a small cell, we can call on any of over 4,000 other white hat groups, if we need them.

Our size means that we can be swift. That we can manoeuvre, attack and defend more aggressively.

That we can easily be replaced and that we can attack and then melt away into the night like ghosts.

When we attack, we will always know the thing we are attacking. We will always know what attack posture we will form and at what stage of the battle. We will always know at which point we could be at greatest risk and what defense strategies we will put into place, whichever scenario unfolds. Prior to commencement of battle we will devise a plan, drawn up in collaboration with everyone we need to take into consideration.

During the battle we will monitor the progress of our plan and adjust our strategy depending on the state of play. At the end of the battle we will all review how the battle went and determine where we could have done better, so that next time around we will ensure that we do much better.

We never do battle with the black hats without first confirming that our target is a black hat and we never mount operations against a target where our resources are better utilised elsewhere. We always prioritise our targets because there is no sense in taking out a small fry target, if our attention could be on a bigger fish. Quite often if you take a big fish out, lots of little fish are taken out too.

So we do our homework. We choose who to target and then we draw up a plan and execute it.

We never take risks so great that we could be taken out of the game ourselves. Instead we prefer to retreat, bide our time and go again later on. We cannot allow ourselves to be taken out. We always consider the bigger picture that we must protect ourselves today, in order to ensure we are available for many more battles in the future.

We always consider the position and actions of our team mates at any point in time. We rely on each other for special skills and we need to know that we can call on each other when we need to. Our unit fights both individually and collectively, but when the chips are down, this elite force turns into A SINGLE RELENTLESS FIGHTING MACHINE.

Intelligence Acquisition

We cannot afford to mess up. We cannot afford to choose a target and take it out, only to find that it was an innocent party. This is where we ourselves will have crossed the boundary between white hat and black hat and find ourselves on the wrong side. We cannot allow ourselves to take so much power and then use it in clumsy and meaningless ways. It matters not to the victim whether we applied this power in an innocent way or in a cunning and deceitful way. What matters to them or their loved ones is that we have used this power against an innocent citizen. We cannot afford to lose the confidence and respect of those who we seek to defend.

So we take very seriously the special powers that we have. We are beyond the ego-minded, beyond seeking to impress friends by what we have learned. By the powers we have over ordinary citizens (OC's). There can be no place in our group for those types of people. There is just too much at stake to let such thoughts enter our minds.

When we strike, we will have spent many days, if not months scoping the target, acquiring intelligence about it from as many sources as we can find. Some of this information will have come from spies embedded in the target domain, other information will come from the public domain, such as newspapers or websites. Other information will be acquired through any number of covert intelligence sources.

As this information is acquired it is assimilated and vetted by different members of the team, depending on the nature of the content. If the information is technical it is likely to be checked by our engineer (Sykes), if it's a location issue it will be checked by a navigational expert (Smouth) and so on. As a group we all help to acquire this information and we will help to assimilate it and then consolidate it so that we have one big picture of what we're dealing with.

It's important that we check our sources regularly, given it is always possible that the black hats have switched a trusted source for one of their own - thus ensuring we are given the wrong information and subverting our intelligence.

Once we have checked our sources using various agent vetting techniques and gathered all the intelligence within the time allocated we are then in a position to test the overall body of information gathered to ensure that it is as accurate as possible.

We will agree on a plan for testing the information and then each of us will devise a method of finding out whether it is accurate or not. Our methods and the results of our analysis are always made available to other members of the team.

Once we have confirmed that the information is accurate we will all agree and signoff the information as being valid at the date of signoff.

Having the information signed off by the team is only the beginning. We still need to decide whether the target in question poses a significant risk and to determine the level of threat we are dealing with, so we can decide, if, when and how we should remove it.
Even If we decide to proceed to exploit stage we still need to evaluate the potential impact of taking the target out and the possibility that our intelligence is flawed.

In the event that we have a green light on to go ahead, we proceed to develop our attack and defense strategies and plan the exploit down to a minute level of detail. Our intelligence processes are always under review given we are always learning. We understand that we can never become complacent. There is just too much at stake. We can't afford to mess up.

Attack Strategies

When you look out into the world – what do you see? People, buildings, the sky, the stars, the sun and the moon? White hats see all these things too, but we also see the strengths and weakness patterns that lay hidden behind the wallpaper of everyday life.

Once our intelligence acquisition, our creative visualisation exercises and our covert operation plans are complete, we pause again to consider the best way to approach the target. We take the information and simulation results and the knowledge of our own position and we begin to evaluate the target even more closely. From this data we produce a set of maps so we can more easily assess how vulnerable the target is and the opportunities it has at its disposal for posing a threat. Vulnerabilities are weaknesses that place the target at risk from attack. Lack of sleep is a vulnerability which places us humans at risk from feeling ill etc.

Opportunities are those resources, knowledge and abilities that the target has at their disposal, in order to counter or launch an attack on an opponent. Vulnerabilities and opportunities are catalogued from top to bottom in order of priority. Understanding where the target is most vulnerable is important to highlight given this will be a major factor in where to begin our attack. Understanding where the target has greatest opportunity is also valuable, given this will enable us to better prepare for a counter-attack in the event that the target decides to use additional resources to launch an assault on us. When the TARGET MAPS are drawn up we are able to identify where their weak and strong points are. Identify where we should strike the blow and identify where and how they are likely to counter our attack.

Once we have identified our targeting strategy, we decide on the tools and techniques we should use for delivering the initial strike (or the payload) and which attack strategy is best for delivering the blow that finally intrench's the target: THEN WE ENGAGE THE TARGET AND ATTACK!

We hit the target with our payload attack
We counter any payload coming back from the enemy
We hit the target again if need be
Then when we know the beast is wounded
We hit the target with our second wave of attack
We hit the target with our intrenchment attack
We counter any payload coming back from the enemy
We hit the target again if need be
Then when we know the beast is dead
We investigate how the battle was fought
And record everything we learnt
There are literally thousands of different types of attack, counter-attack and intrenchment strategies in existence. All as potent as each other. All serving a particular purpose, depending on the nature of the attack.
There is no attack strategy as powerful as the Hydra droid!

Creative Visualisation

When we enter the ZONE, we see everything in Cyberspace.

We visualise the unfolding battle from inside the Zone.

Inside the Zone we run simulations of battles yet to come in our minds and play them out to determine the likely outcome. Outside the Zone we use a battle simulator program to enter the details of our opponents, the terrain, potential battle strategies and then we run our program to create a report on the likely outcome of each type of battle scenario. We use the results to help us draw up our attack and defence plans. After the battle we compare what actually happened with what the program told us might happen and then we update the program to make it calculate more accurately next time around.

We never rely on the program entirely; we just use it to lend extra weight to our plans. Our battle simulator program is simply a computer database which stores millions of records of intelligence patterns representing different forms of hacker behaviour that we have come across in battle in the past. We are always adding new patterns, as we come across or visualise new ones.

In addition to battle and attack strategies, we have developed a program for simulating the mind of a black hat. We use this when we ask the question "what would this black hat do in this type of situation?". This program enables us to see right inside the predators head and to know the potential moves they could make. Again when we know the outcome of its behaviour in a given situation we update our program in order to make the predator profile data more accurate. In the same way as we use our minds to visualise new battle scenes, so to do we use our minds to think they a predator. We ask ourselves. Given we know about this predator, its history and its behaviour – how would it perform when in this situation or that?

This creative visualisation process of thinking like a predator and the behaviour patterns that result from it are used to update our PREDATOR PROFILING DATABASE. In addition to simulating the strategies and tactics of our opponents on the Internet, we visualise our own actions. As a unit we are bonded by many years of working together for the same cause. We believe in each other because we have each seen what each is willing to give up for the cause. But we are all mindful that any one of us could someday become compromised by the black hats and be forced to cross over to the other side. We have sought to reduce the impact of this happening by never revealing our true identities to each other.

Such is the importance of keeping the team together that we have developed a program that contains profiles or each member of the group, along with records of the types of behaviour exhibited in any given situation. We use this program to match the behaviour of our team members with the historical record in cases where one of us is behaving out of character. This gives us the warning signs to take action when we need to. I'm glad to say that we have never needed to use this system.

Noah is the administrator of this system.

Creative Visualisation has been an extremely valuable technique for us in all sorts of ways. From visualising battles in the future to understanding the mindset of the black hats to even assessing risks within our own team.

But we have used it in many other areas, from visualising the kinds of tools we could build to working out how best to share our knowledge with others. Even to entertaining the group from time to time and as a way of motivating everyone to keep on with the fight, by using symbols and metaphors to encourage everyone into action.

Defense Strategies

We know when we are weak. We know where we are weak. We know where they are likely to attack us. We know they out number us. We know if they concentrated their forces at our targets long enough we would be wiped away in a short time.

For this reason we never remain still. We are never in one place long enough to become a good target. With us, there is no fixed reference point. There is no team on a grid.

There is only a target and then no target.

TARGET THEN NO TARGET.
TARGET THEN NO TARGET.

Our defence lies not in the installation of brick walls and firewalls, but in our ability to remain fluid, like phantoms in the wilderness. We are neither here nor there. Neither Spirit nor form. Infiltration is not an option even if a fixed reference point is acquired, GIVEN WE SEE ALL IN OUR PATH. We never interact in a way where we can be corrupted. We never utilise the services of anyone unless we remain hidden.
There can be no danger of infection given there is never anything to infect. As the dust settles so we move on.
When the beast strikes at us, the most they strike at is one of our tails. If there is ever a time where they score, then the tail detaches and we attach a new one and move on.

We can never be beaten in any world because it is the spirit that carries our message and creates the will to fight for the cause to save humanity from the evil ones.
If any other form of defense be required then let those who need one beware that what they try and protect is surely at great risk.

For fixed bricks and mortar and infrastructure of any kind are easy prey to the black hat mercenaries that operate at the heart of the underworld.

Let every man and woman be empowered to defend themselves. Let every citizen be capable to operate at a more enlightened level.
To operate the defence strategy of:
TARGET THEN NO TARGET. TARGET THEN NO TARGET.

Then we will all give the beasts a run for their money.
Then they will be challenged at every point of entry on the Internet. Educate the citizens to fend for themselves and the world will have a greatly more powerful force to go up against them black hats.
THEN WE WILL ALL BECOME LIKE GHOSTS ON THE INTERNET.
WE WILL HAVE BECOME SURVIVABLE SYSTEMS.

Chapter 8 – Hacker Tools – by Sykes

Proteon

Burden us not with technology that we cannot fully see inside. That we do not fully understand, except for what we can see on the surface. Burden us not by the incompetence of these systems and with cheating us to own the responsibility for their erroneous behaviour. Burden us not by their security flaws and the feeling of being helpless to remove electronic threats to our personal freedoms. Burden us not by the growing dependence we build on those who cannot protect us, because they do not make their technology safe and secure. Burden us not with building our confidence on things that are outside our control to influence. Burden us not by the words that a bad workman always blames his tools. These words are folly, for good work can only ever be done when the worker is provided with the best tools to do the job. In such monstrous times as these, when technology threatens to steal our independence away from us. To de-mobilise our lives. How can we sit by and watch whilst it does this? How can we sit by whilst our independence is replaced by a computer that sometimes does what we want and sometime crashes and dies?

As hackers we believe that technology is here to stay and that we too must continue to embrace it. But our belief is that - WE MUST EMBRACE IT – NOT IT US!

We believe in the WAY OF THE WARRIOR. We build our own tools. We build tools that allow us to understand what is going inside and outside the computer. Nothing comes in and nothing goes out without us seeing it and understanding what it is doing. We are both the driver and the mechanic. We are in tune with our tools and we know how best to make them high performance. We know how best to bend them to our will, for we will never bend to there's.

Our computers are slaves to us. Not us to them!

There is a machine codenamed Proteon. It is a machine that does not burden the owner. That does not require a brainwashed victim to drive. That does not seek to subvert the user into becoming an ignorant zombie, controlled by its mystery. Its power. Its implicit threat.

This machine is the machine that can be built from the ground up, layer upon layer. This is the machine that is totally transparent and that teaches you everything about itself as you construct it. This is the machine that when complete, is the one you have most control over. A machine that has no secrets. A machine that reveals all to you and that you have absolute mastery over. A machine that you can pull apart at any time and re-build at any time. A machine that you can add to at any time, without compromising the trust you have built up in the main body. A machine that is the best fit for you.
This is the machine that equips all hackers with the confidence that technology can only ever act on their behalf. That it will not impose any limitation, that it will not translate what they say and that it will not subvert their words or actions, by regulating their communications.

Proteon is the machine we use.
It is the one that draws us into to the Zone. It is the one that gives us eyes through the command line. Gives us the freedom to move through the command line. Gives us insight into the ways and activities of the black hats. Gives us the confidence in our actions. To see everything that goes on. Whether expressed by our action or that of others.
It is the one that equips us best for the challenges ahead.

FOR THOSE WHO ARE TRULY THE MASTERS OF THE INTERNET :-
PROTEON –
THE TRANSPARENT COMPUTER IS THE WAY!

Scanners

Our number is small and the enemy is everywhere. Their eyes and spies in every corner, influencers and power crazed foot soldiers serving the serpents at the top of the pyramid.

Our group moves rapidly, moving freely in and around the black hat monster. Yet our number is small and there is only so much we can learn. Yet we need to be well informed, because there is so much at stake.

Our machine is open, our words are open, the Internet is open. All that we need is more eyes. More minds analysing the posture and movement of the black hats.

These eyes and minds we have sought to create through artificial means. Night and day in the backrooms we design and construct tools that are our eyes, our minds, our alert systems. Night and day we seek to increase our number by building scanning machines. Programs and devices of such simplicity, yet absolutely invaluable to our cause.

When we sleep, our electronic alter-egos are still seeing, sensing, touching and reaching out at the next target. When we fight they are still learning the target, watching its posture, ready to alert us of any change in behaviour.

Scanners that have been produced in the image of the hacker. Ghosts that appear, then disappear. Studiers of targets, harvesters of knowledge, informers of intelligence.
Able to scan in the most difficult of circumstances. Where the terrain is complex, where the walls are high and where there are enemy agents everywhere. These covert scanners cannot be seen, cannot be traced, cannot be undone. These are the ghost scanners, the ones that bring us news as evil unfolds.

Do you know who to trust on the Internet? Do you know what to trust on the Internet? Which targets can you deal with? Which targets are best left alone?

Execute a FOOTPRINTING SCAN and you will find out all the information you need about the target, in addition to where its vulnerabilities lie. Once the footprint scan is complete, the scanner will give the target a trust rating and categorise the target as one of the following:

Unsecured target, Untrusted target, Trusted target
Trustworthy target, Untrustworthy target, Foreign target
Local target, Anonymous target, Spammer target
Very Active target, Unknown target, New target, Old target

Once we know from the footprint scan what type of target we're dealing with, we run a MINING SCAN to delve deeper and to learn more.

Hackers use 100's of different forms of scan, but the best practices for scanning should always be upheld.

You should never execute an investigative scan that brings the target down.

You should never execute a scan that uses only one technique for scanning. Always use multiple techniques for scanning and compare scan results to ensure scans are consistent.

You should never execute a scan that can be traced back to a single machine. It is always best to run scans from different host computers and have the scan code self-destruct once the scan report has been generated.

Transparent & Private Speak

There is a time to speak openly and a time to speak privately.

This is the right of every human being on this planet.

Learning to balance the two is key to safeguarding humanity. There is a time for privacy when words need to be said about our personal lives that we only want certain people to hear about. Private things like about how we feel about someone or personal things about our bodies, emotions, family or homes. There is a time for openness whenever what you say is not private, is not personal, is not emotional and is not expressing feelings for one another.

There are many who use privacy to hide their covert agenda from others. To remove any evidence of their corruption and collusion. For them privacy is a cloak behind which they hide their devilish intentions. They present as honourable men of high integrity. When in actual fact the reverse is more often the truth.

Shame on you bad beasts for if you truly represent truth and justice, you would ensure that what you say is available for all to see. Do not pretend that there is just too much for society to lose by giving up such information, when it is you and your brethren that have the most to lose from revealing the truth.

So privacy is what it means [personal, emotional, feelings]. It is not for hiding the truth, sweeping it under the carpet or subverting our freedoms. It is not for hiding the information we should all be privy too. It is not a tool to be used to mask dishonest behaviour.

Stand up you bad beasts and reveal who you are by using open communications.
--- OR FOREVER LEAVE THIS PLACE ---

Let the workers know what the employers are doing.
Let the employers know what the workers are doing.
Let the citizens know what the government is doing.
Let the government know what the citizens are doing.
Let governments know what other governments are doing.
Let there be open and honest communications in all areas that does not deal with personal communications.
With personal, emotional or feelings.
Let companies defend themselves from the competition, not by using privacy as deception, but by ensuring that they are more competitive and in so doing give the consumer a better deal.
Let citizens know that they must be prepared to speak openly. To reveal themselves, if they have nothing to hide.

When we speak, we speak openly. We operate as if our words had already been intercepted. As if our plans had already been compromised. This ensures that we can be open and that whether we have been compromised or not, our plans will go ahead. We don't rely on our words. We don't rely on our comrades. We rely on the cause we fight for to see us through our battles.
When we speak privately to our loved ones, we use tools to speak in images, ASCII symbols, with embedded messages.

If you cut and paste this symbol and increase the font size from 1 to 10, this sign tells a very different story.

Some of the embedded ASCII text says : "I will be - you know where - at at 8pm".

Black Magic

When in Rome, live like the Romans, think like the Romans, be and act like the Romans. Don't squeal and shout that you are different, that somehow you are better, that you cannot bring yourself to speak or look like them.

If you want to be the best, live with the best. If you want to defeat the worst, then you must learn to live like the worst, be like them, think like them and act like them.

Poison words, magic potions, abuse, murder and subversion are all that excites the minds of the black hat. For these are criminals who use life as a board game.
To connive and to win, all at the expense of those less fortunate. Those less informed. Those who were behind from the day they were born.

Be not afraid of their power for their strategies are easy to see. Their tactics and methods are simple when exposed to the mindset of the hacker. These tricks of mind become a joke when the trick is uncovered for all to see. Its power is dissolved when the illusion it serves is unmasked.
Fear not for the black hat ways can be turned back in their faces. For too long they have been the transmitters of evil. Their minds only tuned toward abusing others by their deeds. Let them now feel the turning of this evil back unto them. Let them see the reflection of themselves. Let them feel the pain they have caused others and in so doing evaporate the ignorance that they have become servants of. Let them understand what humanity has had to endure by becoming the receivers of everything they serve.

FEAR NOT – FOR WE WILL TURN THIS EVIL BACK UPON THEM SO THAT THEIR SOULS CAN BE FREED FROM THE BACKWARD CAUSES TO WHICH THEY SERVE.

Yes my friends, it matters not that we were behind from the day we were born, that our fathers were imprisoned by the ignorance and servitude of their generation. What matters is that we will take the knowledge of the black hats and turn it back upon them.

Consider the behaviour of the Trojans, the worms, the virus's, the data interceptors and the information tamperers and you will begin to understand what forms of black hat tools are waiting to devour us all. Learn their ingredients and you will be endowed with many insights and abilities which you can then use to fight them back.
But know that these ways are dangerous and that you must never use them unless you yourself are in danger. Unless you are prepared to sit back and watch the abuse of those who's cries are never answered by any one else.
Unless there is no other way of safeguarding the victim.
Let the ugliness of their ways and methods be exposed to all.
Let they themselves be exposed for what they do.
Let those who present as the defenders of liberty, serve to stop these criminals succeeding in their quest.
Let those who supply the technology, stop supplying it until it is honest and secure.
Let those who know and dare, stand up and be counted and take responsibility for exposing these black hat bullies.

Stand up and break the strangle hold of these serpents before it is too late. Before the world is completely painted black and then there will be no ability to breathe, no ability to see and no ability to lead humanity out of the darkness.
SAY NOT WHAT YOU DO
ASK WHAT YOU COULD DO
ASK WHAT YOU COULD DO TO DELIVER US FROM EVIL
When your intentions be pure
Use the black magic tools of the black hats to defeat them.

Psychological Operations

Learn not from what you have been told, but from what you know to be true in your heart. Never be blinded by the words or movements of anyone or anything that you have never identified with before. Never be influenced by anyone who suddenly calls you their friend. Never think that there is such a thing as a free lunch, for whether you succeed in getting this thing for free or not, there will always be a price to pay.

True happiness lies in working hard, being true to your word, fighting for what you believe in and finding joy in everything, whatever your circumstances in life.

What you hear and see is quite often illusion, lies and propaganda. Most of what you hear and see is only one side of the story. To gain a balanced view and a healthy outlook on life you need to open your heart and mind to other views. In some cases learn foreign languages, learn new computer skills and get out of your bunkers and meet people on the streets and learn their ways.

Never be sucked in by the hype of the moment. Always consider things carefully. Learn to develop your own sense of independence so you don't have to spend your life having to listen, believe in, or endorse the views of others. Views where there is very little evidence to support the case they make, yet they insist that you take their side. When in your heart you know that these unfair expectations of you are likely to mean they are untruthful people.

We have seen many who present as trustworthy and impartial judges crumble under the weight of the black hat movement. Men who at one time or other speak as loving and honourable leaders of the people, then turn away from the people, turning into cowards who tell lies, manipulated like puppets as their fear had slowly overcome them.

Those black hats who control such activity are some of the most powerful people on the planet. These are the disciples of the devil. The trusted lieutenants of the darkest one.

Watch their faces as they revel in the power they have accumulated.
Watch their faces as they take pride in touting the unknown. Of manipulating your sub-conscious mind to make you dance before them, like cattle on hot coals. Such beasts can only be defeated by playing the same game as them. By applying the same kinds of jiggery-pockery in their minds, as they would do unto us.
Look away my sons and daughters from your TV sets
Look away from your video games, your Internet machine
Away from those who seek to confuse you by their words

Now open the true channels to your mind, to your heart!
Begin by sending your soul into a deep relaxed state Your breathing deep, your mind and your body at peace
This is the place where you can truly begin to know
To visualise the challenges at hand
To weigh solutions to problems clearly in your mind
To see, discover, evaluate and meditate on all things
So that you will trust in the judgements you make

One day when you have developed
the "Way of the Quiet Mind",
You will be able look back again at your TV sets, your Internet machines and your games systems.

You will know who to listen to and who not too
You will know how to take a balanced view of life
You will know how to control those who seek to intrench you
You will know how to look at all sides of a problem

Then you will know that you can trust your own heart to make the correct decisions, form the right opinions and execute good actions, both inside and outside the ZONE. Until that time you must realise that you are not ready to take action, to make judgements and to allow yourself to become influenced by anyone or anything.

You cannot become a White Hat unless you can see the dangers ahead of you. You cannot because to become a White Hat you need to be able to be strong enough to not be influenced by anyone. Wise enough not to be influenced accidentally, by your own miscalculation.

Until that day you must wait and learn.
You must realise that unless you are able to become informed through meditation and education on worldly matters, that you will never be strong enough to live the life that we lead. You will never survive the journey.

Take up the tools of meditation first
Take up the tools of open education
Take up the tools of independent thinking
of Independent Living
Learn how to listen only to your heart
To develop the Way of the Quiet Mind
Then join the White Hat movement
and put your new found independence to work

Be not like the Sheep, be like the Lions head.

Social Engineering

Much of our work is conducted at the command line. Much of our time is spent in the ZONE, watching, waiting and carrying out exploits on those who threaten the good people of cyberspace.

There are times though when we need to operate outside the ZONE. When intelligence can only be acquired from those on the outside, or when we need to concentrate on tackling a physical target, rather than an online target.

Many predators spend almost all of their time attacking citizens outside of the ZONE, or trying to gain influence over them so they can target them better when they're inside the ZONE. These predators give themselves titles like "Social Engineer", when in fact all they are
- are modern-day con-men, tricksters and cheats.

More often than not we need to employ the same underhand strategies as they do. More often than not we need to do this to acquire information that is critical to our mission. More often than not we must play the same games as the very people who are set up in business to cause disorder - the so called "social engineers" themselves.

It's all too easy for them to play out their agenda and there are literally thousands of different ways to exploit anyone from employees to charity workers to politicians. All you need is to think like a crook and you can achieve almost anything.

I know what I know
I know what I don't know
But I don't know what I don't know

{Present tense}

These so called social engineers are able to hypnotise you in to believing that they are trustworthy people. That they are great and likeable people to deal with. That they are in control and that you can be sure that everything is going to work out just fine when they are around. They can help you to become anything that you want to be. That your worth is because of them and when they are around they make you feel just fine about yourself. That in times of crisis they will always be there (even though when you look on the surface they are the ones who caused the trouble). They play on your desire to help others by always requesting you to give up new and important information. Under the guise that it is for some ethical purpose. Sometimes you get a little suspicious and for a time begin to lose faith, only for them to surprise you and then everything is fine. Everything they do and say seems perfect and everyday you like them more and more. Even though you've only known them five minutes. They seem to be able to read you. To understand your needs profoundly. As if they have always known you. Almost as if they knew you more than yourself. You have similar beliefs, they seem to know the same people as you and they always seem to be able to charm you, especially so in the bad times.
Sometimes they bring bad news which makes you angry, but they always seem to be able to get you out of a hole. Sometimes hope and opportunity seems scarce, but they always seem to be able to raise your spirits, as long as you do this or that for them. They say they prefer you when you're acting naturally and taking things a step at a time.
At times you've felt like your losing your mind.
Things you should have known, but didn't. Even things that you did know that you couldn't remember.
Strange....strange.....strange.
Don't trust a stranger. Listen to your heart.
Listen only to those who you know in your heart to be true.
Those who have stood the test of time and remained true.

Chapter 9 – Hack Anatomy – *by Smouth*

Defined

We hack because the intelligence we need can only be acquired through hacking. We hack because most of the people who are in the corruption business are hacking to achieve their aims. We hack because we can and because it is a cheap and fast way of getting the job done. Of taking the black hat regime out.

In its simplest form a hack is a story, an adventure, a journey into the unknown, a mission embarked upon for one or a number of causes. A hack is both concept and action.
A hack is something you think about and then do to the end. A hack can be as simple as using a neat idea to get lots of people to your website, to writing some code that creates a backdoor to a computer system, to producing some great artwork that encourages everyone to think more creatively.
Hacks are simple ways of achieving goals using smart, new methods, rather than existing methods. Of course a hack can be used for both good and bad purposes. Hacks can be used to create nightmares, as well as fulfilling dreams.
Hacks are created by people who can manage to perform the hack, from start to finish.

Our own hacks are conceived and recorded for entry into a disclosure database. When a particular action is required, the activity can be matched against a known hack pattern and then the hack is executed. If there is no hack in the database which matches the required action, then it is necessary to dream up a new hack.

Hacks can be spilt into three main categories
1. Hacks that are in the public domain
2. Hacks that are unknown
3. Hacks that have not be released in the public domain
Number 1 is simple. These are the hacks that we can all see everyday, if we were only to open our eyes.

Number 2 refers to those hacks that have been executed, but have not been identified as yet.

Number 3 refers to hacks that white hats like ourselves have already executed, but within a closed test environment.

It is also possible to categorise hacks into two areas which relate to the type of outcome of the hack:

1. Hacks that cause threat(s) to the target
2. Hacks that create opportunity in the target

Number 1 refers to the kinds of hack we use for fighting the dark side of the hacker fraternity. Whether we're gathering information or striking the target, we're conducting a threat orientated hack.

Number 2 refers to hacks that once executed cause the target to have greater potential. If we were to socially engineer a member of the public in order to ascertain information to be used to protect them, then we are conducting an opportunity orientated hack.

In the future, the major battlefield will be fought between those hackers who have the greatest ability to produce new and powerful hacks. For it is the newness of hack, the uncertainty of them, the unknowing of them that gives them their power.

If you want to be an elite hacker, you need to start by thinking up and building at least 2 new hacks a week.

If you want to be an elite hacker, you better start using your mind for things other than day dreaming, watching the TV or playing computer games all day.

You need to start thinking about how you can produce hacks that deliver justice and freedom from black hats.

And those that empower people into leading a life of peace, fulfilment and harmony.

Adventure

Every hack has a beginning, middle and an end.
It also has a purpose for being created in the first place. This purpose is usually something useful. The more useful the better, given your hack will be rated by the value it brings.
Are you going to produce a "Threat" orientated hack or an "Opportunity" orientated hack. Are you going to hit a target to create a threat or an opportunity?
Which one is it?

There are those who believe that hacking has an additional category, the "Educational" orientated hack.
They believe that exploring for their own personal knowledge should allow them to hack into any computer they find on the Internet. To play with other peoples property. To aimlessly go wherever they want, just so they can supply themselves with the utmost information.

For what purpose? For whose gain we ask?
To hack for education is not a bad thing in itself, but to hack someone else's computer system is. There are plenty of computer shows out there to purchase old equipment and hacker clubs where you can learn and get educated in the ways and methods of the hacker, without having to resort to testing your skills randomly on unsuspecting and innocent targets. Indeed, sometimes the target will not be so unsuspecting and as a novice hacker you may be more likely to find yourself in hot water than anything else.
Much of what you hear of hackers today is about people who are caught breaking into computer systems and then thrown into prison.
These sensationalised stories serve to tarnish the name of the good people in the hacker community. To demonise the term hacker, so that the black hats can keep the white hats down in the eyes of the people of the world.

Pick an adventure, create a hack. Create a beginning, a middle and end, then work your way into adding the detail. Work out the beginning and the end first, then get into the middle and then add the rest of the hack content in there.

Start
Once upon a time there was this group of black hats that kept publishing copies of our computer games.....

Middle
We built a distress code generator into our games so that we could tell where the people were who were playing copied versions of our games, so we could contact them and find out who supplied the game to them.

End
After contacting over 100 gamers, we tracked the pirates to an address based in Hong Kong. We contacted the police and got them closed down. The ring leaders were arrested and then thrown into prison for 5 years.

Then fill in the rest of the detail from there.
If the hack makes sense, make it work!

Most hackers give their hacks a unique number, starting from hack#1 and so on. You can even give your hack a prefix such as using the initials of your name. So if your name was John Smith, your hack might be called JShack#17. You can even catalogue your hacks, by the type of hack, the type of target it can be used on and the value it brings.

That's all there is to it. Start designing your hacks today and then find out how to make them work.
THEN MAKE THEM WORK!
MAKE THEM SERVE A GOOD PURPOSE!

Target Model

Hacks are executed against different types of target.
Targets can be people, computer facilities, objects or organisations of any kind. Each target has a number of common elements, these being assets, controls, vulnerabilities, threats and constraints.

Outside of the Zone, The target (them) is known as an "player". Inside the Zone the target is known as a "user".
The source (us) is also known as an "player" outside the Zone and again a "user" inside the Zone.

Every player has an objective, which they carryout by attacking and defending.
Every player has a cause, a purpose for which they fight.
When a hack is executed, an incident is said to have occurred. This incident is likely to be reviewed by the victim in more ways that one.
Each side has both an attack and defense strategy and a security plan for ensuring they keep their house in order.
The battlefield upon which they fight is known as either the "threat domain" or the "opportunity domain", depending on what type of hack they are executing.

Regardless of which type of hack, every target has assets and controls, vulnerabilities, threats and constraints.

Assets are the physical objects, ideas and information that you are trying to protect or to destroy. These assets are usually kept safe by any number of security controls. Security **controls** also provide facilities for launching attacks against targets. These counter-hacks can be either threat or opportunity orientated. Your assets are always vulnerable to attack given there will be weaknesses in them that make them less safe. Security controls are designed to protect these **Vulnerabilities**.

In all walks of life there are **Threats** and you will find that your assets are no less at risk from threats than anyone else's.

Finally, every asset should adhere to certain standards of security. Either from the government, or your parents or your employer. By ensuring you secure assets to this standard, you are ensuring that you are complying with the **Constraints**.

Basically what this all means is that you (and your target) are a bunch of assets that are protected by security controls. That include some vulnerabilities, which open you up to threats and that you must ensure that you reach certain security standards so you can be seen to comply with the constraints.

Every asset can be said to be at risk from danger, to one degree or other. Some assets might be at risk to threat orientated hacks and some may be at risk to opportunity orientated hacks.

When a target is engaged this may cause an alert, it may not.
When an exploit on a target is executed, this will usually cause an incident that will need to be investigated.
This investigation can trigger a counter-attack against the perpetrator of the exploit and/or a recommendation to improve the security controls so this type of incident never occurs again.

Once the incident is closed off it is normal to review what happened at a later date, just to ensure that nothing was missed at the time and that lessons had been learned from this incident!

Hack Types - Threat

For hacking exploits that typically involve intelligence collection these can be split into four distinct stages

1. Blueprint the target
2. Gain access and mine for detailed information
3. Create back door in target (easier access next time)
4. Cover tracks

For hacking exploits that involve an offensive attack on the target they can be spilt into four distinct stages

1. Blueprint the target
2. Gain access and mine for detailed information
3. Attack the target
4. Cover tracks

Further patterns of attack may be required and further exercises to cover your tracks may be required.

The initial stage of an exploit hack is to discover as much information about the target as possible. This stage is called Blueprinting and involves **Footprinting**, **Scanning** and **Enumeration** of the target. Footprinting refers to conducting a non-intrusive investigation of the target.
This is a high level assessment, designed to find out as much information about the target, using information available from publicly available sources, such as websites, libraries, newspapers.

Scanning refers to a non-intrusive investigation of the targets entry points. These entry points are then used to mount an intrusive form of assessment called Enumeration which involves gaining access to the target using some of the key entry points and security privileges, then acquiring deeper information about the target.

Once you have gained sufficient information in order to be able to **gain access** to the target, you can then work on how to **escalate privileges** in order to gain a higher level of access to the target and expand your scope of control by **exposing mechanisms** that will gain you access to other trusted systems.

In the case of intelligence-collection orientated threat hacks this would be the point where we may have acquired all the information that we need, at which point we might create a backdoor into the system and then cover our tracks.

Creating a backdoor involves installing invisible doors in the target so that when we want to gain access again in the future, that it is a much simpler and much safer task. **Covering tracks** involves removing any evidence that we ever gained access to the target.

In the case of an offensive attack orientated threat hack, once the relevant information has been acquired we would then attack the target and then cover our tracks.

Attacking the target involves selecting an asset or a number of assets within a target that need to be removed or partly reduced and then applying any number of payload or intrenchment strategies to take out or subdue the target.

Once the attack is complete, we will cover our tracks so that we won't leave any evidence behind of our presence.

It is important to note that information is often acquired to identify the most vulnerable areas of the target. This is done so the perpetrator can more effectively concentrate their attack at the weakest point in order to get the fastest and most effective results!

Hack Types - Opportunity

Opportunity orientated hacks differ from threat orientated hacks in that you the user are not looking to threaten the target to destroy it, but to exploit it to increase its value.

Value can be measured in many different ways including happiness, motivational, educational, protection, performance, health and efficiency.

With Opportunity hacks you can actually make people happy. You can motivate people to make them do the things they want to do better. You can get them to think better and improve their education and you can help to make performance improvements in people and things.

This is the style of hack that white hats prefer to use every time, although we use both types for obvious reasons.

Quite often we mount an operation using an opportunity hack, knowing that if the nice approach doesn't work that we will need to apply the nasty approach (a threat hack) to get the job done.

Again, there are four distinct stages to conducting an Opportunity hack.

1. Blueprint the target
2. Gain access and mine detailed information
3. Assess Opportunity Gaps
4. Deploy Value in Gaps

Again, the first two stages involve investigating the target to the level that you fully understand who and what you are dealing with. Unlike the threat hack you are really acquiring information for purposes of helping to add value to the target, as opposed to destroying or reducing it.

In this case intelligence acquisition is quite different because we are attempting to understand the weaknesses in the target for purposes of filling them with value, as opposed to causing damage and mayhem by exploiting them.

To a white hat, everything is a target of one form or another.

Once we have fully understood the target, we assess where there are areas inside the target that are weak or not optimised. Where improvements can be made and where changes would produce significant results. These weak areas are then listed down in terms of those that would produce the maximum results at the top to those that would produce lesser results at the bottom.

Once the list is complete we decide which weaknesses to exploit and then apply value to the target accordingly.

Some opportunity hacks include,

Ethical hacking – where a security specialist tests for system weaknesses with the sole purpose of plugging gaps, thereby saving the owner time and money.

Workgroup hacking – where there is a problem with people getting along together so the hacker assesses where the weak links are in the group and then works on these people to inspire them to change their behaviour so that the weakness goes away and the group work better together.

Self-Confidence hacking – where people have no belief in what they do, so the hacker identifies what is limiting their confidence and works to eradicate it, so that people get an honest reflection of themselves upon which they can build.

Performance hacking – where some performance problem exists, an opportunity hack comes in handy.

Chapter 10 – Hack Example – by Jaqs

HACK#17 FOREWORD
Excerpt from Tomb of the Game Testers Hack #17:

Many hackers think hacking is a technical exercise. Few consider the art of hacking to be an exercise in creative problem solving. That hacking involves the alignment of many more factors, from technical design and social engineering, to information warfare, predatory psychology, experiential design and cyber-visualisation.

For most elite hackers have skills that ensure that whatever they do aligns all these factors so that the hacks they perform are amongst the biggest and best hacks the world has ever seen. It means that hacks need not be as simple as carryout an exploit on a single target, but that hacks can be designed to mount large scale attacks on a greatly more sophisticated enemy.

Think a hack that takes out a target, or intercepts someone else's credit card details to be a major hack? Think that a denial of service attack is a major coup or that Trojan you've managed to embed in the target? Think that breaking in to national defence computer systems is the cream of all hacks. Well think again!
What you must remember is that the majority of hacks today are conducted against sitting duck targets. Devices that are always immobile, just waiting to be examined. Just waiting to have their vulnerabilities scanned. A sitting duck target, just ripe for exploitation.

In reality the most challenging targets are never immobile. Never static. These targets are always moving and relentless in pursuit of their agenda.
The really great hackers are able to hit a moving target, better than most average hackers could ever hit a stationary target.

SUMMARY OF STORY

Every hack mission we embark upon has a beginning, middle and an end.

Hack #17, "TOMB of the Game Testers" is an example of one of the major hacks that we have been involved in over the past 7 years.

Hack #17 was a mission to stop a group of black hats taking over a video game network run by a team of game testers, located in Southampton, England. The hack we mounted was in direct response to a level 4 incident that we were alerted to by a black hat turned white hat, agent, Cibermole.

Level 4 incidents are caused by RealWorld agents who are in the process of infiltrating an organisation for purposes of gaining some degree of control, usually to serve some selfish agenda.

Our scanners detect evidence of a DEADZONE on the video game network and our investigation leads us to identify where the likely black hat threat is coming from.

In order to establish the facts we need to collect detailed information and essential video evidence.

Once we are clear who the perpetrators are we draw up our plan, share out the responsibilities of who is going to do what and proceed to execute our attack.

Our plan then gets foiled by one of the assailants and we need to take them out of the picture for a day or two, to give us a chance to target the remaining black hats.

Our new plan is activated and results in the removal of the primary black hat and the expulsion of the rest of the group by the lead game tester and his team.

Our post-mortem revealed that had we executed the hack differently that we would have managed to avoid detection the first time around. A decision was then made to take a different approach on level 4 incidents in the future.

BEGINNING (OUTLINE OF HACK#17)

Elite Game Testers aren't just ordinary gamers. These guys aren't hobbyists or tournament entrants or world champion enthusiasts. These guys are 24*7 hardcore testers. These are the guys that test the games we all play each and every day. These are the guys that hack the game code hidden beneath the game. These are the guys that live and breathe the game. The guys that are part man and part machine. Part loving, caring human-being and part shoot-em up warlord or champion football manager.

The guys who when all have gone to bed are still working on their game strategies for tomorrow.

But these guys don't just play the game like gamers or build the game like programmers.
These guys are in the business of breaking the game!
Play the game against any of these guys and you are not going to last 5 minutes. If they can't beat you in the game they'll make sure the game ceases to operate, by working a few tricks that sends the game to sleep. They know every twist and turn of the game, because they spent 10000 hours testing it, from the time it was born and submitted to the lab, to the numerous versions leading up to release.

You'd have thought these guys were immensely powerful!
You'd have thought they would be capable of repelling any form of hacker attack!
You'd have thought that they had all the right tools!

That's why we were really surprised when we were alerted to a major level 4 incident at the game tester lab in Southampton.

A level 4 incident is the second most severe attack you can get. It is so significant it can damage people for life.

RealWorld Agents are the elite troops of the black hat order. They are masters of disguise and deception. They are field operatives and spies who are usually on a mission to infiltrate the target in order to steer it towards becoming a fully fledged black hat operation. To turn it from white to black. RealWorld Agents work from both outside and inside the Zone. Once we had established that there was more than one black hat operating inside the organisation, holding a senior position, it was no surprise that the testers had been unable to remove these sinister forces. Doing so might have resulted in them losing their jobs. Possibly losing their identity by being thrown out of the gamer space that they know and love each day of their life. It would have been too much of a risk for them to take.

This problem was clearly not going to go away on its own as the creepy DEADZONE created by the undermining Black Hats continued to spread throughout the game networks.
To penetrate the testers minds and to lead them away from the lightness and towards the dark side. Blackmailing them into joining the ranks of the dark knights.
By hijacking their minds, by threatening to take their life of computer games away.
It was our duty to eradicate this scourge. To remove it without damaging the experiences of the game users.
Without destroying the reputations of the online game testers and without revealing our own identity.

Our plan is always based on solid investigative work.
Our plan is always jointly owned by the team.
We know what we have to do.
Who the target is.
What the strategy is.
Now all we have to do is attack.
And trust that the battle will be over quickly.

MIDDLE (OUTLINE OF HACK#17)

As we pursued our investigations, we uncovered more and more evidence of the black hat conspiracy that lay at the heart of the organisation. Our agents infiltrated the game networks through the electronic systems and placed the targets under constant surveillance.

Our intelligence scanners acquired all the evidence we needed to justify mounting an attack. Our intelligence lead us to believe that such was the graveness of the situation that we must act quickly and decisively. We decided to take the target out, given that you can never reason with devils of this kind. They are simply far to well indoctrinated to be able to turn them away from the darkness. Certainly we didn't have the time to do this anyway. We had to move quickly.

We are covert agents. We never want to carry out an exploit in such a way that our presence is felt. In such a way that someone would be able to say "WE'VE BEEN HACKED!".

In such a way that the target would have no reason to believe that their plight was anything more than an accident, a slice of fate, something that was meant to be.

We move like ghosts and our acts are like ghosts.
Well they should be!!

Our error was that we tried to reach out to another. To inform someone covertly that there were villians operating inside the organisation. When in actual fact this other person was so well possessed by the beasts that all information in and all information out was allowed to be seen by the eyes of those who had influenced this man.

These RealWorld Agents were alerted to our presence and their response was to close off access to the systems whilst they continued to devour it from inside.

We needed to change our plan of attack. This wasn't going to be so easy now.

Our backdoor we installed earlier is the only way in now.

It was lucky we put it there. Lucky we follow procedure.

We knew that the black hats were extremely intrenched in the organisation. We knew that it would be difficult to remove them, without doing damage to those around them.

Our initial plan was to remove the black hats by exposing their plot to everyone. It is clear that this would be a waste of time given that everyone in the company had already become brainwashed.

We decided that the only way to remove them, was to somehow get them transferred out to a different mission. To get them to leave this place by their own accord and ply their evil trade in a different part of the world.

Our plan was to lure the black hat leader away by creating a different problem nearby that he was compelled to attend to. Then to expose and discredit the rest of the black hats whilst he was away, in order for them to be overcome and expelled by the gamer testers.

We pinpoint the gamers who are most likely to stand with us.

Our plan is drawn up. We know how the hack will work.

We know who is responsible for doing what.

On the eve of the battle we prepared by reaffirming our collective commitment to ridding the world of blacks hats.

Of eradicating them at every opportunity, so that humanity will someday be free and that only love and peace and freedom will rein over us.

END (OUTLINE OF HACK#17)

Our secret weapon is our leader and agent Cibermole.
To influence a black hat, you need to understand their language. To understand their language, you need to be one of them. You need to think the same way, behave the same way, know the same signs and symbols, enjoy the same pastimes and ultimately fight for the same causes.

Black hats only trust a particular form of behaviour. If you don't exhibit this, then you are not one of them. They can tell from a mile off whether you are one of them or not.
Cibermole was born a black hat. Born in to a family of elite black hats. He was given no alternative, but to follow the black hat order. But instead of supporting or resisting them. Instead of walking away or challenging them directly, he has chosen to fight them from inside. To quietly subvert their causes. To work on the other side, whilst carefully carrying on the pretence that he is one of them. What is more, Cibermole is one of the most elite of black hats, so he knows more about what is going on than most ordinary black hats. So when all else fails against a black hat. When electronic forms of hacking become ineffective, we use the authority of Cibermole's position to get the job done.

All that is needed sometimes is a word in the right persons ear for a chain of events to occur which arrives at the right result. Its quite amazing how the dominos fall with never a trace of who or what set them falling. Never an obvious source of blame. Sometimes it is incredibly difficult to follow a logical path back to anyone who can be blamed.

A whisper in the ear of a tier six black hat results in the transfer out of the senior black hat to another unsuspecting part of the world.
Somewhere near Siberia, we were given to understand.
 thus splitting up the group!

With the senior black hat out of the way, the rest of the team set to work to reduce the stranglehold of the remaining black hats. We needed to convince the man in charge of the game network that the remaining black hats were up to no good. This would then convince him to expel them and to realise that the senior black hat had also been up to no good to. Thus resulting in them never being asked to work on his game network again.

Our plan was simple. It involved getting the gamers on our side. Helping to build their confidence, so that when the time came they will be brave enough to fight on our side. We laid a trap, just like the predators themselves. It involved setting the bait. It involved causing a problem, waiting for a response, then offering a solution that would result in the eventual expulsion of the remaining black hats. This method is called PRS (Problem-Response-Solution).

We understood that one of the black hats plots was to gain greater influence over the manager of the network. They didn't want to remove him, he was a good cover for them, but they were seeking to gain influence over him. One way they sought to do this was to gradually weaken him in the eyes of his online game users.

One way they sought to achieve this was to contrive to slow the game down. They did this by tinkering around with the system, in the small hours of the morning.
When the game went slow, they were always the ones who could speed it up again, giving the Manager the impression that they were very important people to have around.

[CAUSE A PROBLEM]
Our group recorded the keyboard activity of the early morning hacks. We then altered the script in order to cause an error so the lead game tester would be alerted that a hack had been perpetrated.

[WAIT FOR RESPONSE] Further investigation by the game testers provoked a response which involved alerting the manager to the hack.

[OFFER A SOLUTION] We drew his attention to a vital piece of evidence, thereby exposing the perpertrators.

This got the rest of the black hat operatives expelled!

Our group conducted a post-mortem on hack#17, which confirmed our initial mistake in alerting the black hats.

We changed our operating procedures.
An error we would never make again.

Chapter 11 – THREAT NETWORK – by Cibermole

Perpetrators

On the frontline of the black hat forces are the perpetrators. The gatekeepers of the net who have been cast in a role to intrench humanity. These are the multi-level droid signatures that serve to subvert and to wage war on all good things.

Sinister forces sent to put mankind on a collision course toward self-destruction.

These demons stand side by side plotting and engineering the downfall of man. Twisting, tricking, slowing and discrediting everything they come into contact with.
Always following the agenda they serve, never questioning its substance, its motives, its intentions.
Always moving in alignment with its desires.

These grotesque creatures come in all shapes and sizes and have many different capabilities. Some have tiny impact, some significant enough to undermine the progress of mankind. All are part of the threat network that has been set-up around the globe.
There are five classes of Perpetrator, level 1 posing the least significant threat, level 5 the most significant.
1. Bugs
2. Virus/Trojans
3. Droids / Handlers
4. RealWorld Agents
5. Alien Masters

Each of these categories of perpetrator are capable of carrying out an exploit on a target, causing an impact to one degree or other. When the black hats move against a target, they select which type of perpetrators they need for the battle and advance on the victim in a formation which probes and attacks in the most efficient way.

Whatever strain of perpetrator you are facing, all can be identified by a unique signature pattern. When we search for threats on the network, our scanners alert us to the form of threat, its location and the number of targets already infected by it.

Sometimes we find many different strains of perpetrator at a specific location which means our own attack patterns have to be very carefully tuned. It is usual for black hats to install a series of booby traps, so that if one perpetrator gets exposed, the rest automatically self-destruct, taking everything else out. That's why we place so much importance on careful planning.

Careful planning = quick and effective attack = success
Poor planning = slow and ineffective attack = failure

When we unravel the grip of the predator, we want to make sure that we do it in a way that doesn't create more of a problem than we had at the start.

Some perpetrators are operated by other perpetrators. Some are programmed to operate on their own. Some are human, some are computer based. Some move fast, some move slow. All seek to collaborate to perform their sins.
The one thing they all have in common is that they are all ruthless predators who seek to serve an agenda which follows the ways of the evil ones before them.
To continue to follow the ways of the black hat order. People and things who have anointed themselves CHOSEN ONES when in reality they are really the FALLEN ONES.

The evil ways of those who have hidden the truth from billions of people for thousands of years do not need to be understood.
These ways just need to be disposed of, that's all.

Bugs (threat level 1)

Sure, it's a bug! It's no ones fault! An accident, a freak of nature! An omission even!
"Anybody can make a mistake mister!"
Sure, that's what they want you to think.
"SOMEHOW I JUST DON'T THINK SO!".

These insidious critters are much worse than they seem.
In fact there are many who believe bugs are the worst ever, because what masquerades as a fault in the system, or an oversight by someone, is in fact more often than not the act of a predator with the most deceitful of all intentions.

At least when you lock horns with a virus, you know its come to try and smash your face in. With a bug, you just never know.
In any case, if they were manufactured by accident (like bugs apparently are) then who takes responsibility when they go off? Who is going to clean up the pieces?
Worse still, who the hell knows where to find them, are they hiding under the floors or walls – where the hell would they be? Do you know where these things are? What form these bugs take? What they can do to you?
Have you ever been surfing the Internet, only to find that your PC suddenly doesn't respond anymore? That you've been rebooted into a black hole or that your game characters are missing parts of their heads or your Internet connection has gone walkabout? What about that bully who just had a go on your MP3 player, which doesn't quite work the same anymore! Seemed a bit wet when you got it back - didn't it? Now it's really full of bugs.
Well they're bugs. Mysterious things (apparently) that go bump in the night. Things you least expect to occur.
Things that suddenly happen, cause you grief and there is very little you can do about it, with no one seemingly to blame for it.

Errors, omission, inaccuracies, invalidations, incompetence's, incompletes, faults, failures, accidents, conflicts, incompatibilities. All of which are types of bug.

Worse than the devil you don't know is the devil you really don't know. Bugs that are produced through human error are one thing, but bugs that are introduced into the mix by the black hats, is quite another. Bugs that can be attributed to the source, the person who introduced it, is one thing. But bugs that have no owner, with not ability to trace them to the producer is a real problem.
There are many incidents where black hats have got jobs as computer programmers in firms for the sole purpose of introducing bugs in the software. Many of these bugs turned out to be back doors that have been inserted in the software so that when installed the black hat could gain access to the owner's computer system. Imagine if your own computer software had been infiltrated by this type of bug. How safe would you feel right now?
It is said that some people introduce more bugs than other people. They say "he's prone to introducing more bugs".
Well what these people should be asking is, "is he doing this deliberately?" or "is this guy just not very good at his job?". Either way, he is a menace.
The black hats use bugs in almost every attack they make. Mainly because they cause bad things to happen and there is no way the source of the bug can be tracked to them.
A bug can trigger a seemingly unrelated sequence of events - another reason black hats like bugs because the greater the number of events that preceded the final devilish act, the harder it is again to pin it on anyone. Next time someone says "it's only a bug", pause, then think about what they're saying and ask "Are you sure?" "How can you tell?"

Then, look for the people who most likely introduced it?"

Virus (threat level 2)

Is it a worm? Is it a Trojan horse? Is it a cannibal, a vandal, an infector of things, a hoaxer, a spammer, a ruthless marauder? What is it?

"Just what the hell is it that is slowing me down?"
"Where are all my files gone?"
"Hey, why is my hard disk light flashing - and I'm not actually doing anything?"
"What do those alert messages mean?"
"Why does my machine take all day to boot up?"
"Why didn't my anti-virus program stop that infection?"
"Hey where's my CD drive gone?"
"Damn popups, just can't get rid of them!"
"Now I've got to reinstall the machine again!"
"Maybe I'll go and purchase some more security software – perhaps that will stop this nonsense!"
"OR PERHAPS I SHOULD JUST CHUCK THIS COMPUTER IN THE SEA!"

Black hats are masters in the art of destroying your computer experience. Of taking advantage of your lack of knowledge and then stealing from you, smashing up your software and then trying to discredit you in the process.
Many of these people spend all day writing strains of virus's and then sending them out into the wild.

Virus's take the form of computer software programs that have been written in such a way to infect other files, thus creating more carriers of the virus and spreading it to other files on your computer. An infection that goes unnoticed can spread very rapidly and cause untold damage to thousands, if not millions of computers. It goes against convention but we classify any computer instruction code that has been sent to subvert your computer as being a strain of computer virus, irrespective of how it performs.

Black hats make a great deal of use of Trojan horse virus's. When one of these finds its way on to your computer, it means that other people can gain exactly the same level of access to your PC as you can. In effect the Trojan horse opens the back door to your PC and the black hats can walk right in.

Another type of virus is the Worm and this is one of those nasties that wiggles its way around other peoples computers, quite often stealing information or simply creating havoc and destruction, wherever it goes. You can get virus's that set logic bombs to go off at a particular time, virus's that can replicate themselves all over the show, virus's that when detected can change their signature making them harder to detect and virus's that check your email and maybe send a few bogus messages to people on your address list. And there are zillions of other forms that will each eat you computer anytime for breakfast.

Most virus's are made up of three parts.

[Part 1] Each has a way of infecting a target computer. The virus checks if the target is already infected and if it is not - it infects it, with a copy of itself.

[Part 2] Each virus has a trigger that is used to indicate when it is time to deliver its attack. So the computer virus on the infected computer will be waiting for the trigger to alert it to do its evil deed.

[Part 3] Each virus has a payload stage which executes the payload, which can be anything from sending rude messages to your friends, to eating you computers hard disk.

If you want to weaken a target, create mayhem or simply break in and steal everything people ever worked for, become a black hat and get into virus making. Apparently its fun and you can spend many a happy hour reading about how the virus you wrote wiped out half a million computers. How you created a virus that caused distress to people and untold misery to people you will never meet. Like people who are old and frail. A performance you can only ever dare to share with yourself. Enjoy it! Live with it! Or just, grow up now!

Droids / Users (threat level 3)

Every dark key press is another piece of the monster. Another movement, another dastardly act. Like a living nightmare, orchestrated by the hands of the cloaked users. By those who seek to share with us only the parts of themselves that are evil. To share their demented behaviour through the keyboard and out onto the Internet.
Creating biometric droid signatures that crawl around delivering the worst kinds of venom.

Fear not for bugs and virus's, for these droids are the things that undermine the human soul of the Internet.
Droids constructed by black hat key presses.
Droids that can deliver bugs and virus's in an instant. Droids that can close down websites and intercept money transfers. Droids that can close the Internet down and make the world a less safe place in an instant.

Touch the keyboard and behold a droid is born. Press the keys in a particular order and watch it dance before you. Work, work at becoming a professional keyboard presser and your droids will become greatly enriched.
How many years have your fingers touched the keyboard? How many of those years were spent pressing the keys in constructive ways? In ways where your mind is learning new techniques for attacking and for defending the target?
In ways where your are exploring new worlds and educating yourself in the ways of the programmer.
Black hats have studied these ways for many years. They have not directed attention to watching TV, playing video games or spending time in idol gossip.
These black hat users are the real thing and you will find that the droids they produce, are evidence that they have been spawned by some of the best minds in the world. Minds that have absolute mastery over their craft and absolute commitment to their cause.

Where there are groups of black hat droids attacking a target you know that the target is in real trouble. Every droid will operate a very different attack strategy. Each will approach the battle from a different dimension, yet each will understand they fight, united in formation, in the name of the black hat cause.

There is worse still to tell. Over the past 10 years black hats have been developing automated Droids that can operate without key-pressers. Droids that are made up from recorded key-presses. Key-presses which are stored then played back without the key-presser needing to be present. Recorded droids that can alert the user when their assistance is required.
That can operate whilst the user is asleep.
That can fight on behalf of the user.
That can never be traced back the human who sent it.

Some droids are like autonomous agents.
Level 3 of the threat pyramid includes all droids, whether by key press or automated key press.

This level also controls level 1 and 2 threats.

L5: Alien Masters

L4: RealWorld Agents

L3: DROIDS / Users

L2: Virus/Worms/Trojans

L1: BUGS

RealWorld Agents (threat level 4)

Level 4 of the threat pyramid is inhabited by those who use their every being for the cause. Those who use more than fingertips and hands to spread their evil. Those who are as committed to the black hat order as you could ever be.
These are those who put themselves in danger every minute of every day. Those who would put both their physical body and minds at risk to fight for the cause.

These are the real-world interactors. Those who appear warm on the surface, yet are icy cold inside. Those who appear to totally committed to your agenda, when in fact they have always followed their own selfish aims. Those who smile, when in fact they are laughing at you. Those who would appear to stand at your side in battle, when in fact they are just about to stab you in the back or to walk away. Those who are there, yet not there. Proper, yet not proper.

Yes these are the true agents of the devil. The social engineers, the double agents, the integrators of deception.
These are the people who control level 1, 2 and 3 of the threat pyramid. Those who are seen, yet not seen.

Do you know anyone who fits this description?
Anyone who you have never been able to work out. Someone likeable, yet you have always been cautious of. Someone who appears perfect in every respect.
Almost too perfect.

Well beware for they may well turn out be a RealWorld Agent. Sent to undermine and influence you. To acquire important information from you or to embed themselves in your heart for many years, until activated in some way.
Beware, because these are the intelligence agents of the black hats. Beware of them, for they wish harm upon you.

Sometimes these RealWorld villains need to call on the services of the underworld on the Internet. Sometimes they need the services of the droid masters. Sometime they need the services of those who can manufacture bugs and virus's.

For these are those who will use every object, tactic and strategy know to man. Whether it be in the real world or in the virtual world.

Masters of disguise, creators of illusions, conjuerers of black magic, the RealWorld Agent sets to work against the target. Smoothies, Charmers, Gossipers and Diplomats, they impress their evil ways upon an unsuspecting audience.

Who owns them, nobody? Who instructs them, nobody?
Who controls them, nobody? They are of their own making, yet by chance happen to follow the same path as the highest of all black hats. The Alien Masters.

Alien Masters (threat level 5)

There are those who fight and there are those who are the cause of the fights. The ghosts that pull the strings of the living. The ghosts who for the past 3 thousand years have been creating an illusion that many call the Matrix.

Those who would set men against men. Nations against nations. Those who would create fear and poverty to serve their own selfish agenda. Those who create the illusion of creating good, when in reality these good acts are used to trick the minds of the living and ultimately become a stepping stone toward absolute mastery and control over mankind. Those who have distorted history so that the reflection of the present is what they want it to be.

Are we living free people, or are we cattle in the bull ring of the Matrix? Yes, the top level of the threat pyramid is inhabited by a tiny master race of people who are ultimately responsible for the design of every entity in the Matrix.

When the time is right they manoeuvre those in the threat matrix toward a new target. They direct them to deliver their payload in all the right places at all the right times.

What appears as coincidences, mysteries and accidents is in fact evidence of sharp practice and collusion. The Alien Masters direct their battalions through mind control. Not even their own followers are aware they exist.

Seek to unravel their deeds and you will spend a lifetime in the task. For they have minds that are greatly more enlightened, because the world they see is very different than the world you see. That's because the world they see, is in fact the real world.

The world you see is in fact an illusion they have created for you. The illusion that your parents will have unwittingly painted for you.

It is the illusion of limited possibility.

The Visual Mind Prison (VMP).

Those who are overpowered by the VMP illusion become a pawn on a chess board. Your every move tracked. Your every action recorded. Your every decision made for you.
Believing that your actions are a direct result of decisions taken by your free will is pure fantasy.
In actual fact you move as a result of fear and anxiety, herded like a sheep by those who use the subversive tactics of the Visual Mind Prison to manipulate your mind.

Yes, these are the darkest of all knights. The most powerful people on earth. People we never see or hear about.
People who have such an effect on us, yet we never understand why they do this to us?

Is it any surprise they hide their faces from us!.
What would happen if mankind found out what they had been up to and came knocking at their door.

Yes, the most powerful piece of the pyramid is also the weakest part too. If the demons at the top were ever exposed the whole nasty thing would come crashing to the ground.

Then the truth about them would come out. Then the people would begin to ask the questions that they are programmed not to ask today. To challenge what we have been told about our history so we may find real peace and truth in the present.

For these beasts serve only one agenda and that is to control humanity through a single world order. When the world is one, then they will have arrived at absolute control and mastery over mankind and the world will be marked by only one sign.

"SIGN OF THE BEAST"
- NO WAY OUT!"

Chapter 12 – VISUAL MIND PRISON - *by Noah*

Attention

There are those who believe that the Visual Mind Prison is created outside of our minds and then we are all lured into it and become trapped. That mankind is unable to solve this problem because it no longer has the tools to perceive what is happening to it in the first place.

That some external force has stolen our imagination, replacing it with the images it wants us to see.

Rendering us vulnerable, incapable of defending ourselves. That we are all being controlled by world events and that we are all doomed and that there isn't much we can do about it because the enemy is not something we can control, see or touch. That our understanding of the truth is limited by our own imagination, which has been re-programmed by the Alien Masters since the day we were born.

There are black hats that crawl this planet. Many of them more powerful than you can ever believe. Many of these people would like to take control of the world. Would like to round us up like cattle and herd us into some fascist controlled bullring of limited possibility.

But the reality of it is – THEY CANNOT.

Many have tried but have been unable to break the spirit of man and so long as this remains true and strong they will never succeed in their ambition. For as long as there is one single white hat on this planet, the black hats will never defeat us. For we know their flawed agenda and we will tell it to the people. We will tell it to their hearts and they will know again which direction they must take.

The complete meltdown of humanity will come not from some black hat threat but by mankind falling into a total dream state. Caused by becoming intrenched in the things we have created for our own amusement.

Caused by the things we have designed to make our lives somehow more bearable. Hypnotic things like technology, media and drugs. Caused by mankind becoming lazy, unconstructive and docile. Caused by humanity losing its independence, its freedom, its confidence and its joy.

No my friends, the threat of becoming intrenched by the Visual Mind Prison comes from within, it does not come from any enemy outside.

Once you understand how powerful you truly are, you will realise that the ability to take control is really within your grasp. AND YOU MUST TAKE IT, LEST YOU FORGET WHAT YOU HAVE LEARNED AND FALL BACK INTO THE ABYSS.

Attention is what the black hats seek to steal from you.
For when your mind is pointed toward directions of limited possibility it will not be attuned to the things that really do matter. Things like saving the world from annihilation. Like developing the mind and body of a warrior, preparing to defend truth and justice. Like sharpening the mind to bring peace and love to mankind, rather than sitting idly by whilst you watch the vultures pick the bones of the weak and less informed souls.

Control your reaction to mass opinion and emotion. Clarify every issue. Be the master of every act. Concentrate on the task at hand.

Direct your attention toward the things that really do make a difference in peoples lives and you will never become a prisoner of the Visual Mind Prison.

Concentration

There are no better exercises to help you concentrate on becoming a free spirit than immersing your mind in Zone. For the deeper and longer you remain in the Zone, the stronger your concentration will become. After a while you will not be distracted by the noises around you. By the other voices in your head. By the facile duties you need to carry out for others. You will simply see the hacks as they are played out before you. Totally immersed in the business of becoming a white hat.

Once attention on becoming a white hat is obtained, concentration takes over.

It begins with the command line. Simple and basic in form. An interface that lets you perform. An interface that gives you the control, the confidence in knowing that everything you see and do can be understood. That you are part of a world that channels your energies and desires and enables you to see the best of yourself. To do work that is truly remarkable and that is representative of your true potential. To truly be able to contribute to mankind, through the medium that is the keyboard and command line.

What do you feel like when you've got nothing to do? Nowhere to go? No idea of what you want to do? No belief in yourself, watching others achieve success whilst you sit idle? When your disillusionment leads to anger, frustration and gets you into trouble? When you feel you are wasting valuable time watching TV and playing computer games. When you are getting fat and out of condition, never having the motivation to doing anything about? When you don't feel you belong? What do you do? What do you do?

You need to get some direction in your life. Get involved in something you believe in.

Step right up; take a leap into the unknown. Don't be shy!

Get concentrated and join the army of white hats and do real things with your life. Take a leap into the Zone.

But be not under any illusion that unless every step is taken in service to humanity, then no good will ever come from concentrating your mind like the white hat. For motive is all important in doing what we do.

You must be sincere in your belief in defending and protecting others against evil. You must be clear that you want to become a warrior of the online world. You must be clear that you want to turn against evil and that you are committed to the end. Committed to hacking for the rest of your days.

Never let yourself become negative, for negativity will eat away at your will to live the life of a hacker.

Never let yourself become arrogant and self-congratulating for pride and vanity will eventually expose you as an hacker.

Never let yourself follow Gurus and psychic illusions for they will trick your mind into coming under their control.

Never let yourself live the life of a hacker, if you will it not, for you will not be a willing servant and you are better off using your body and mind in others ways.

Never let yourself neglect your exiting duties to your friends, family or employers, for this is your connection with reality. This link you must maintain all your life. Without it, you could lose yourself entirely in the Zone and and open yourself up to becoming consumed by the VMP.

Always, stay real, because that's what you are - REAL!

Always, make sure you surround yourself with good people.

Always seek wisdom, not power, for wisdom is to healing what power is to destruction.

Always seek pure motive for doing good. For motive is behind action and if you are sincere in your belief for doing good then you will truly be doing good by your actions.

Pure motive toward doing good is where the life of a white hat begins and ends.

Identity

Want a new identity? Want a worthwhile identity? One that really makes a difference to people? The sort of difference only valuable members of the community can make?

Want to wake up every morning and know where you belong. What it is you do with your life. Where you perform. What it is you do to contribute.

Want to know that what you do, you enjoy. That what you do is worthwhile and something you can do all your life.

Want to cast away the wasteful hours that lead you to go nowhere and create an identity that takes you everywhere and to be anything you want, at any time?

WELL STOP WASTING TIME, LIVING IN A DREAM WORLD, BEING DISTRACTED BY EVERYTHING AND EVERYONE AND GET INTO THE WHITE HAT SCENE!

Education can be great, but wouldn't it be even greater if it were served up in more interesting ways?
You know – like hacking!!!!!

There is nothing I can learn at school that I cannot learn leading the life of a hacker. No place I cannot go.
No thing I cannot see and everyone is online, so I'll never be alone. I know who I am. I know what I am here for.
I know what I'll be doing tomorrow and next month and next year and for the rest of my life. Know what I'll be wearing.
HOW ABOUT YOU! Well forget not knowing who you are. Blowing in the wind, waiting for something to happen.
Get a hacker ID.
Sure the VMP is always there, but when I'm not consciously ignoring it, I'm hacking the sad arses behind it.

You got to know that the VMP is a creation of our fathers and their fathers before them. It is an illusory world that stops us from realising our true potential. Leaving it behind is essential and the way you do this is to get control of your mind by stepping into the Zone. There you will know who you are and for what purpose you serve.
People will say, "hasn't he changed."
"What's up with him?"
"He's always so preoccupied these days"
"Never seems to be off of that computer"
"I'm not sure what to do with him"
"I can't get his attention"

"WELL, HOW ABOUT SHUTTING UP!"
"I'M TRYING TO SAVE THE WORLD!"
"WHAT THE HELL ARE YOU DOING WITH YOUR LIFE?"
"EXCEPT WORRYING ABOUT MINE, OF COURSE!"

Ok, so other people don't like the term hacker.
It seems that the more ignorant you are about life, the less you understand about this word and the more hostile you are towards it. Unfortunately those who are most able to educate the uninformed are usually the ones who are least able to reveal who they are. Such are the laws of the white hats.
It just wouldn't be smart to reveal who we are.
That's just plain stupid. The kind of mistake that others have made in the past and found themselves in jail for making.
Sure, when these guys are released from prison they end up on some TV show, or worse still, writing a book.
But who the hell wants to be seen as a failed hacker?
Who the hell wants to be a seen as a failed black hat who now masquerades on TV as an enlightened white hat? Even if all they ever were in their hearts, was a white hat!
People can know who we are, as long as they never know what we are.

Reality

Reality is not a Stalag 9 concentration camp.
Reality is a beautiful rich place where the occasional villain must be brought to justice.

It's a place where outside of the Zone we are at peace and inside the Zone we are at war. Where we make few enemies outside, only inside. Where outside we lead ordinary and unassuming lives, but inside we are completely full-on. Where we leave our passion and ferocity at the door when we exit the Zone into RealWorld.

Reality is living between two worlds. Never the twain shall meet. It's about achieving a balance so that you can live effectively in both worlds.
Those who seek to strengthen the influence of the Visual Mind Prison serve to intervene in this process.
Seek to get in the middle of the transfer between RealWorld and Virtual World. To intercept us from moving freely and safely between the dimensions. Using diversionary tactics to lure us off the path, to disrupt the progress of the white hat order.

Think Reality should be a dream world where everyone lies around doing nothing all day? Where you don't have to make a difference? Where you don't have to achieve anything? Well good for you.

We certainly don't believe that!
Reality for us lies in TWO WORLDS'.

One where we rest and share our love and one where we fight alongside our online comrades to reduce the influence of the enemy. A reality where we seek to defend the human race by using only love, thoughts and computers.

WE LIVE IN BETWEEN TWO WORLDS.

WAR   PEACE

ONLINE   REALWORLD

Freedom

What is this sense called Freedom? Is it being able to say and do what you want? Is it having everything you ever wanted? Being everything you ever wanted to be? Living life as you would want to? Having rights? Being respected by others?

Yes, these are the freedoms that you would wish for yourself, but freedom means much so more than that.

It is about respecting other people's opinions, circumstances and privacy. It is about leading people out of poverty. Enabling everyone to have access to education and health care, not just the privileged few.

Above all things it is about defending the basic rights of every human being on this planet and removing those who threaten this cause.

There are many who believe that Freedom is something they themselves can give or take away. That they are the chosen ones whom we should all look to for our Freedom.

People who use Freedom as a weapon for controlling your mind, your body and your behaviour.

Watch out for these dark souls for there is one around every corner. Know that whatever they do or say. Whatever they bring upon you. Know that they must never take away your true spirit. Your true mission. Your true belief that love is everything you ever need in life.

For the beasts can take everything away from you and you will still be there standing. You will still be there, with integrity in tact, with hope intact, with body intact, with mind intact, with honour and decency intact, with intellect intact, with will intact, with spirit intact and with faith intact for now and for all time. Believe in love and the fight against those who move against freedom and you will always be true to the white hat cause.

They say that if they take your computer away, you cannot enter the Zone and therefore you can no longer operate as a white hat. They say if they intercept you for many years and incarcerate your mind in the Visual Mind Prison that there is no way back for you. They say that if you've committed crimes in the past that you can never become a white hat. They say if your mind cannot write programs that you will never make it as a white hat.
What lies, what propaganda, what an attack on your basic freedoms!

There is room for everyone to join the white hat movement. For those who seek to build a world of justice, through self-sacrifice. A world of tolerance for all men and women.
If you do not have a computer then we will find you one. If you have had difficulty finding your way back into the Zone then we will help you. If you need education in the ways of the hacker, then we will help you. If you have done bad things before then prepare to make good on your crimes.
If you cannot write programs then prepare to learn.

It is the right of every human being on this planet to have access to the Internet. If you do not have it, then you will become disadvantaged and so will your children and your children's children.

So get online. Learn like you have never learned before. Read everything you can. Learn how to use your computer for research. Learn how to sell things online. Learn how to find everything you need. Learn how to safeguard you and your computer from virus's and such like. Learn where all the best places for information are. Learn how to write programs that do things whilst you sleep.
Once you get there, we will teach you how you can cultivate even more freedom by joining the white hats.

Chapter 13 – BLACK HAT CULT - by Cibermole

Pyramidians

Pity them, for they know not what they do.
Such a strategy to outwit mankind. To twist and bend humanity for their own selfish ends, is but a flaw in the many fundamental flaws that belie their black hat agenda. For they believe they do this for the good of this or that, when the ultimate aim to create a prison world will never be for the good of anyone. Least of all our children.
And it will never become a reality anyway.
For we will never let it be so.
These men of courage. These men of faith. These men of deluded integrity, believe that the power pyramid they have silently created to intrench us will stand for another three thousand years. That it can never be undone by anyone. That man is too feeble to perceive it. To challenge it.
To prevent its momentum. They believe that the illusion they have created for the minds of the ordinary will disempower them for all time and rob them of their will to live and fight as honest men. To know the truth so that we might all live our lives, both independent and free.
Yes, the computerised threat network at the heart of this movement is but a devious device designed to shape peoples future at every point in their lives. To create the illusion that life is rich, varied and free, when in fact our destiny is fashioned through fear, from the time we first get lured into the black hat trap. To entice and trick us into serving the black hat manipulators that occupy the upper layers of the **Power Pyramid**. At every turn there is a black hat waiting to slow you down, to undermine your thinking, to trick you into believing that freedom lies in giving up your freedom. In return they say they will remove the fear from your mind. Fear constructed and conveyed to us, by people like them. If not by their own hands, this fear creation manifests as a statement of words so profound, so devastating, that its effect is to terrorize people into giving away what their forefathers gave up their lives for.

Freedom from tyranny. Independence for all.
How sick is that? Many of these disciples know not who and what is above them. Know nothing more than ways to stab you in the back. For the elite Alien Masters have created an evil power structure that ensures their agenda can be served without them ever having to be exposed.
Every black hat operates inside a small pyramid that forms a larger pyramid that ultimately forms the complete pyramid, of which the Alien Masters operate at the top. The top point is known as THE ALL SEEING EYE.
From the top, these backward types can control the whole ugly agenda to take over humanity.
They are aware of everything that goes on within the black hat operation and the more their power spreads, the more they will have access to things that only the most trusted of our leaders should see. They seek to infiltrate every part of our society in order to control it. They seek to gradually erode the confidence and trust between men. To seed fear, uncertainty and doubt in the minds of both the weak and the strong. To trick them into giving up more of their rights to basic freedoms, blinded by illusions that are played out before them.

One day you too will serve the beast.

Yes, many of these barbarians are at the heart of power already and we must hunt them down and remove them.
Always beware of the clubs for the rich and famous. Of qango's that serve some hidden agenda. Of agendas that are unfounded and appear unsound. Of groups who speak in several hundred tongues. Of those people who pretend that you understand them when they clearly know you could not.
For in these groups lie much corruption and if they are not already Pyramidians then they are surely fertile ground for becoming so.
Watch for the ego-minded leaders for these people know more than they are letting on. Watch for the premadona's who expect all men to fall before them, unaware that their posture is that of the devil. The ones who believe they are the chosen ones. The ones with the education. The ones whose flesh and bones has somehow more right to be alive than anyone else's. Those who think that the art they create is somehow of value to mankind, when in fact they are deluded.
Paint squashed on canvas, noise in the air, smells and tastes, all less art than one single act of one simple man in the service of mankind. Beware of the Visual Mind Prison, but behold the unveiling of the true enemy that lay within.

Open your heart and you will know who they are.
Seek out the PYRAMIDIANS and expose them.

Plot

Forget going about life blindly, being and doing this or that. Listen to your heart, trust it, follow it.

For the heart is the guiding light instiling in each and every one of us a sense of intuition, leading us to uncover more of the truth.

Leading us to a life of ever unfolding enlightenment.
To understand their moves. To know their game.

Look only at the architecture of their play, the true nature of their ways, the intentions behind their action.

See past the trickery of images, the effects of personality, popularity and enforced movement.

Look for the true motives behind their performance to know how best to engage them.

Or vanish off the face of this earth until you are ready to responsibly adjust the beasts influence.

For good will never come from creating any illuminated adversary of the beast. For where there is competing celebrity there is the illusion that supports a belief system of opposites. Promoting a duality of positions filled with lies and self-serving intentions. Promoting conditions of untruth, mis-direction and unfathomable betrayal.

It is known that the strategy the beasts have chosen is cunning and cuts to the heart of humanity on a scale never before seen. Its moves are pervasive, seeking to pollute our minds by using the Internet as the vehicle.

Its persuasive power is far-reaching, all-embracing.

It begins with the creation of a small network of spies and ends with the absorption of humanity into this network.

It begins in the same way that many cults are started where rules are created for everyone to follow and if you don't follow them you are either chastised or expelled.

If you remain loyal and work hard for the cause then all will be fine and you will be rewarded in some way.

As time goes by more and more people are lured into joining the network and demonstrating its advantages to recruit others. When the size of the organisation outgrows the ability of the Alien Masters to control it, they delegate authority down to their most trusted lieutenants. When the size of the operation outgrows the lieutenants, they encourage conditions whereby everyone in the organisation is expected to take responsibility for imposing the rules on others, so that the pyramid becomes self-policing. In other words, the cult runs itself from this point on. Even to the extent that those at the bottom don't know they are part of a global system, governed from the top. When the regime begins to breakdown or when the masters decide to steer the herd in a different direction or hasten the speed of change, they will use fear and conflict to assert their authority. They can create the conditions where men will fight men for some purpose. For some prize.
For some noble cause. Whilst the men are fighting and the people's attention is drawn away, they instigate whatever changes they like. Changes that hasten their agenda.
Yes, this is what the black hats have in store for us. This is what they seek to draw humanity into.

Know this and you will be able to prepare for it
Know this and you will know the enemy you fight
The signs of the covert ones
The moves of the dark riders
Know this and you will never be ignorant again
Know this, because as a white hat you need to know
For you are good and they are bad
For you are strong and they are weak
For you know them and they don't know you
For your heart will never be there's
It will always be yours
Yours, Yours, Yours
Forever White Hats!

Raptorialis (rap-tory-r-lis)

We are the prey and the Pyramidians the predator.
They wait, ready for the day when we are all plump and docile. Ready for the time when we can be quickly devoured.
The Internet world offers them greater opportunity to advance their agenda, but it also presents them with many dangers. Dangers that also threaten to rip them apart.
As the predators seek the prey, so to does the prey seek the predator. For it is in understanding the hunter that the victim can turn the tables.
Yes, the beasts have created and chosen the Internet as the final battle ground. It is the device by which they seek to speed our race to spiritual annihilation. The mechanism by which we will ultimately submit to a life of slavery.
A life where we are all contained, itemised and remobilised, so that we can serve their evil agenda in ways where we perform without ever being a burden to them.
First comes the technology. Then the programme to build dependency upon it. Then there is the total breakdown of human conscience and confidence as our desire to be free, independent loving human beings is erased from our soul. Resulting in us ultimately becoming slaves to the machines.
Then comes the unveiling of those who dominate mankind, never to be challenged again.
Watch as the plot unfolds before you.
Watch as the beasts reel you in like a fish on a hook
Watch as you are enticed away from free, independent living
Where you are enslaved in a world where you cannot survive
- without the things that you can do without today.
Where your arms and your legs have no purpose any more
No real purpose, except interacting with technology
Where some day your desire to be human will whither and die
Where all you will feel is the whisper of the barbarians.
Tricked into becoming a custodian, a mentor, an advocate and gatekeeper of their power system
- they call The Illuminated Kind.

Beware, these predators have thought to counter those who know and dare to stand against them. Beware for they have many weapons in their arsenal.

Watch and behold the signatures of their ways for they can be simply read, if you were only to open your heart.

Listen to your heart and you will know what moves you must make. Your intuition will never let you down.

The ways of the predator are many fold and they have many techniques for mass manipulation. Watch for the one that is called Fear-Response-Judge, for this is a common method amongst participants in this malign power system.

Fear.Response.Action (For Predators)

STRATEGY
Situation: Need to move the agenda forward but can't get anywhere using ordinary strategies.
Fear: Create a Problem

Response: Wait to see the reaction to it

Judge: Punish or Praise

EXAMPLE
Situation: I need this person to do some dirty work for me, but their good nature won't allow them to do it.
Fear: Tell them they are going to be kicked out of the group unless they do every I say. Inform what you want them to do.
Response: Wait to see their reaction to my request
Judge: If they complied with my request, say well done and you are safe in this group. Or get rid of them. Done.

Vulnerabilities

Know this, that the vulnerabilities of a person are not created by accident, by chance. They are manufactured to create the illusion that you are dependant on someone or something. That you cannot live without the services of those who profer to make you safe. To help you overcome your fears, when in reality they are the ones who cause you to doubt yourself in order to ensure you do what they want.

What would happen if there was no such thing as anti-virus software? What would happen is that the manufacturer who sold you the software that runs the pc's would have to clean up their act because if they didn't, we'd all stop buying PC's and use something else instead.

We're told by the open source community that to be safe we all need to stop using a particular manufacturer's proprietary software product. We're told that unless the code is open, it cannot be trusted and that we are all vulnerable if we don't start using open source software.

Well let me tell you this.

NONE OF THIS SOFTWARE IS TRULY OPEN-SOURCE.

UNLOCKED CODE OR NOT.

HOW MANY PEOPLE DO YOU KNOW COULD EVEN READ THE CODE IN AN OPEN-SOURCE PRODUCT – LET ALONE UNDERSTAND IT?

ANOTHER ILLUSION FOR US TO BUY. TO MAKE US FEEL UNCERTAIN, WITH NO GOOD PURPOSE TO IT.

Truth is, when open-source gets really popular, it too will be targeted by the black hats and rendered unsafe.
If your PC breaks down or your mobile phone chooses to disconnect. Who do you blame? Well you blame yourself of course? You say, "Well it must be because I don't know how computers work" or "I must be in the wrong area for wireless reception". Humbug!
You don't say, this thing doesn't b***** work and take it back like you would the TV or radio you just bought!

Why do you do that? Why do you put up with it, just because it is a different type of technology?

Truth is that we are the real source of our fears.
If we choose to give our independence away so cheaply. To be tricked in to believing this or that lie.
How can we complain that we are no longer in control?

Black hats hate the ones that talk of independence.
They create vulnerability all around them, to reduce them.

But the enlightened man knows that vulnerability is all in the mind and that this mind can be reprogrammed to ignore it. To control it. To never let the fear that if offers bring them down.

BUILD A LIFE OF TRUE INDEPENDENCE AND YOU WILL REMOVE ALL EVIDENCE OF VULNERABILITY AROUND YOU. LET OTHERS TRICK YOU INTO BELIEVING THAT DEPENDENCE ON OTHERS IS GOOD AND YOU WILL SURELY LIVE YOUR LIFE IN THE SERVICE OF THOSE WHOSE ONLY AGENDA IS TO CONTROL YOU.
WHEN FEAR STARES AT YOU, STARE BACK AND LAUGH IN ITS FACE.

FOR FEAR IS THE ULTIMATE BLACK HAT ILLUSION.

Chapter 14 – WHITE HAT BIBLE - by Noah

I_Atom (from white hat bible)
{Use the I_Atom Spirit to understand your true nature}

Why would the book of white hats be called a Bible?
Why would the white hats call it such a thing?
Surely it is only a book of hacks, strategies and insights? No more, no less?
Surely it is no more than a learning book on how to become a white hat?
Whosoever names it Bible?
Whosoever dares to call it by that name?

IT IS NOT WHAT IT IS CALLED. IT IS WHAT IT IS.
WHAT IT IS CALLED, IS WHAT THE WHITE HATS HAVE DEEMED IT TO BE KNOWN AS.
WHAT IT IS KNOWN AS, MAY BE KNOWN AS SOMETHING DIFFERENT IN THE FUTURE.
FOR WHAT IT IS CALLED IS IRRELEVANT.
IT IS WHAT IT MEANS TO WHITE HATS THAT MATTERS.

The "I" is the symbol of the "many into one" and the "one into many". If you were a single atom, then you would view the world as a mass of single atoms and then you would know that you are one of the many and many of the one.

You must know that there is no such thing as variability in life, because everything is predictable.
That we cannot calculate life's happenings exactly, matters not. Everything we do and say is as predictable as night following day and day following night.

Variability is at best an illusion. At worst a lie.

This doesn't mean that you should sit back and wait for your destiny to play out before you. What it means is that you can move forward in the knowledge that what will be will be and that you can be sure that it will all end someday.

If you were meant to be a single atom, then so be it.
If you were meant to be the highest mountain, then so be it.
But be sure to know that pain and suffering can only be erased when those who profer such lies as the existence of variability are eradicated. For their science is founded on ignorance. On supposition and on cavalier miscalculation.
For what is not completely known, should not be used as an opportunity to create flawed arguments for the convenience of those who do not really know. For what is not entirely known, may be beyond the realm of this heavily blinkered generation to calculate.
It is our intellectual pride and our desire to want to believe that we are more than ordinary human beings that tricks us into believing that variability = freedom, when in fact variability = slavery. False knowledge that tricks us into believing that freedom is born from first accepting that life is a place of constant turmoil and uncertainty. That freedom is won only by the special kind who overcome the challenges of variability. When in fact every man and woman in this world has the right and ability to be free, whatever their education, background and ability. All they need to do is open their hearts and realise they can choose freedom at any time. You already are free! Be still, listen! Everything is predictable. Variability is fear in disguise. In reality we are many of the one and one of the many. We are everyone and everything, and everyone and everything is us. There is no variability, everything is predictable. We are all atoms in wavebands and the atoms in wavebands are made all of us. We are all a configuration of each other. Bad nature and good nature intermingled into one. It is for the good nature to overcome the bad nature, so that every man and woman be saved from those who seek to confuse mankind through illusions, psychic phenomena, lies and jiggery pokery. We must use the knowledge of the "I" to see through the illusion of variability and to move us toward turning the bad atoms into good ones.

I_Factor
{Use the I_Factor Spirit to set your mind free}

The strands that bind the laws of nature to the human race are beginning to be pulled apart by the forces of uncertainty. By the forces of unpredictability. By the forces of variability. By the forces of fear. These strands need to be reinforced. Need to be bolstered in some way.

The I_Factor is a way of visualising these strands and enabling humanity to take control of the illusion that is variability. For variability exists only in the mind of man. It seeks but one agenda, to break and to confuse. To cause disjointed, disconnected, disordered and disillusioned lives. Variability seeks to disunite man unto his fellow man. To steal his attention away from his true nature and to deflect his mind toward a collidescope of broken dreams.

It serves only to offer the hand of power to the ignorant, the incompetent and the down right corrupt. It serves only to cause pain and suffering. It serves to spread fear and ignorance. It serves to reduce man unto himself and render him less free in his own mind.

I_Factor means "Intrenchment Factor". Any particular object or group of objects can be measured in relation to how free they are by applying the laws of Intrenchment. I_Factor relates to the degree to which an object (say the human spirit) is in Intrenched.

Whether against its will or not.

To which an object is pinned or not pinned in a particular position of space and time.

It means "the degree to which an object is free, or not free, depending on how you want to look at it."

There are four dimensions to I_Factor
1. Intrenchment
2. Retrenchment
3. Re-intrenchment
4. Detrenchment (in), (re), (rein)

Intrenchment is the degree to which an object is fixed firmly and securely in a particular position of space and time.
Retrenchment means the degree to which an object is becoming less firmly and secure in a particular position of space and time.

Re-intrenchment means the degree to which an object, after retrenching from a particular position in space and time has subsequently intrenched by, relative to its original position in space and time.

Detrenchment means the degree to which an object has been intrenched, retrenched or re-intrenched in a particular position of space and time, through the influence of a third party. Types can be differentiated as follows: De-trenchment(In), De-trenchment(re) and De-trenchment(rein).

If you look at an object in a particular position in space and time (say you), you will note that at any point you are more or less free. This more or less free can be calculated by the laws of the I_Factor. Once you realise how more or less free you are, then you can do something about it.
Use the I_Factor to measure the variability around you, to calculate how free or not free you are.
As you apply the I_Factor, you will realise that variability exists merely as an illusion in your mind.

You will realise that variability is in fact:-
Fear of being frightened, which if you think about it, is an illusion. Such a condition cannot be measured given fear of being frightened is never grounded in reality.
At that time you will have reached enlightenment.
Then you must spread the message to set everyone else free. Help them to see that variability must be dissolved from their mind perspective, in order to set them free.

I_Motive
{Use the I_Motive Spirit to predict the future}

You need to understand the motives that gave rise to changes in history if you are to understand the real truth behind why a particular event took place.

You need to understand the motive, the intent behind this or that force for change before you are able to calculate the pattern of events that will unfold in front of you in the future, or indeed to positively affect them.

For once the motive is established, the degree to which the intrenchment will be or the speed and direction at which it will take can be calculated.

Prediction will be accurate if the motive is known, else the illusion of variability will reign and disorder will introduce itself into the equation.

Whether the motive is good, bad or neutral - matters not.
You cannot predict world events unless you understand the motives that gave rise to them.
Where there are hidden agendas, there will be no visible motive or the motive published will be false. Designed to subvert the process that gave rise to the investigation.

For many men have taught themselves to believe that trusting their fellow man is not a good option, to the extent they throw out lies of their agenda. Or is it their incompetence, pride and ambition that makes them want to hide the real truth. When humanity turns into a caldron of false motives and hidden agendas, then there will be a day of reckoning. This day will be the day when men of all kinds, of all creeds, of all colours, come together for the final battle with the battalions of black knights that have humanity cornered.

I_ATOM

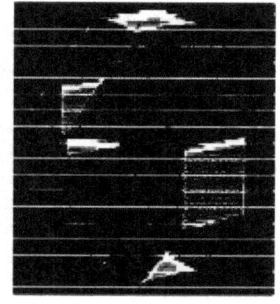
I_MODEL

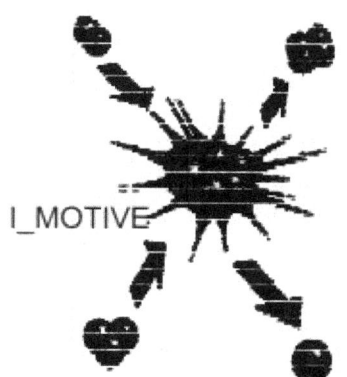
I_MOTIVE

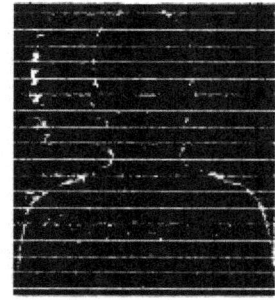
I_HACKER

I_FACTOR

I_Model
{Use the I_Model Spirit to design optimum technology models}

Our world is a model. Technology is a model. Business is a model. You are a model! We and everything has a MODEL. I_MODEL is the strategy, the creativity, the technique that extends and harmonises these structures, forming new systems that greatly advance mankind.

I_MODEL is the art of creating new technology models for aiding humanity, through the integration and alignment of components, intersecting the real and virtual domains.
By using virtual reality characterisation, communication devices and hacker behaviour to improve our world.

We seek to support the I_Model by removing the influences that serve to undermine its progress. To dilute selfish acts.
To unlock what agendas are hidden from us.
To remove that which stands in the way of love and peace.
We must build a world that is open, honest and free.

Of the people, for the people, by the people
Then the white hat I_Model can make a real difference

New technology models must adhere to the laws of Intrenchment. They must be designed to deliver the payload into the target to the level of intrenchment required.
They must be designed in a way they are effectively integrated into the target in sight.

I_MODEL is a force for good, drawn from the fields of mathematics, intuition art, psychology and strategic and tactical design. It is that which conveys right knowledge, strict morality and universal charity. It is the philosophy of uncovering the inner truths of models and the creation of models for the good of everyone.

The continuous search for the beauty of good, the intelligent light that reveals the object in its first created form. In its first created truth. The purity of the form, the unwrapping of the reality that lies at the heart of the model. This underlying morality and truth is exposed by the application of the I_MODEL.

For this is the art of creating models for the progress of mankind. Of uncovering the truth behind the complexity of form to reveal the intelligent reality within. For the purpose of re-engineering forms. Of perfectly aligning the focus of technology models toward serving humanity.

Of seeking to improve the world through the effective deployment of technology devices, in open, unselfish ways.

And to finally realise the real purpose behind the laws of God and in so doing bring freedom and peace to this earth.

A model can be produced in any language. Any communication device. Any component. Any behaviour.

Be they Open, Semi-Open or Closed in ingredients.

Be they free, semi-free or not free.

Be they slow, semi-slow or not slow.

Be they from rich vendor, semi rich or not rich.

Be they integrated, semi-integrated or not integrated.

Be they human, electronic or neither

We choose from a rich unfettered spectrum of choice.

What, where, when how and why

Then we build.

Build models toward PROGRESS, toward doing GOOD.

I_Exploit
Use the I_Exploit Spirit to influence change in the target

Intrenchment exploit strategies are designed to intrench a target by this or that much. Applying these strategies results in a loss or gain to one degree or another. A loss or gain in freedom of the target.

Technology Intrenchment refers to the process whereby technology devices are used as enabling mechanisms to engage, augment and sustain a position relative to a target. "Targets" can be anything or anyone from
"A computer", A network" "An individual", "An organisation", "A marketplace" or "A geographical location.

Intrenchment goals are the mission objectives set prior to launching an attack against a target. These include "remove target", "empower target", "slow target", "subvert target", "stop target", "increase target", "stabilise target", "position target", "reduce target resistance" and many more.

Intrenchment Strategies are the different plans, concepts and patterns of behaviour that white hats design in order to intrench a target. These include, "Just Enough", "Hi-Win First", "Stepping Stone", "Many Faces, Many Places", "Fear-Response-Kill", "Retrench-Self-2-Win", "Infiltrating the Customer", "Mole in the Camp", PSYOPS, EBW, trust vehicles, cats paw and many more.

Intrenchment value is the term used to define the value that is derived from a technology Intrenchment exploit. This can include, "attacker removed", "attacker under control", "backdoor created", "communications intercepted", intelligence acquired" and many, many more.

Intrenchment Dimensions is the term used to define the different factors of Intrenchment, such as Retrenchment, Reintrenchment, Disintrenchment, Counterintrenchment and others.

Intrenchment Applications is the term used to define the different types of intrenchment target. These include "games piracy intrenchment", "social engineering intrenchment", "e-marketing intrenchment", "device entrenchment" and many, many more.

Psychological Intrenchment is the condition whereby a target becomes psychologically intrenched by an exploit.

Intrenchment Psychology is the condition of mind of the designer of intrenchment strategies.

Physical Intrenchment is the condition whereby a target becomes physically intrenched by a target.
Intrenchment Countermeasures is the term used to define measures that the source can choose to counter
an intrenchment attack by an opponent.

When you design your exploit strategy you must use the Laws of Intrenchment. You must consider the disciplines of engineering, integration and intrenchment.
You must know how to hack, design and building models. You must know how to integrate people, technology and processes.
You must know how to deliver in order to intrench the target.

You need to know your target. You need to produce the technical maps and blueprint your target's risk and opportunity posture.

You need to design an exploit plan that will engage, enable and intrench your target.

Then deliver the payload.

I_Hacker
{Use the I_Hacker Spirit to become the most powerful force for harmony}

When you add or remove variability from people's lives, you are making them intrench, retrench or re-intrench. How they react depends on their personal motivation.

Some will react very differently than others. Some will retreat in the face of adversity where others will hold their ground. Where others would strike the enemy before it had a chance to react. In the face of unimaginable fear, most would react the same. Most would cower or flee.

The hacker is that which is best able to cope with adversity. Best able to challenge those who attack using variability.

Best able to combat those who deal in fear and subversion. Because the world of ever-change is what they are used to.

They know how to cope in a world that is unpredictable.

They are best placed to fight in such terrain.

Best equipped to fight the illusion of variability.

To slay it, whenever it rears its ugly head.

They are the most trustworthy under such circumstances.

The most reliable. The most capable.

The most likely to succeed.

The white hat hacker is a builder of tools, of techniques, of strategies, concepts and exploits. The white hat hacker is a skilful lean machine that turns the payload of evil back in the faces of the destructive ones.

The white hat hacker is a visionary, a defender, an inventor, hacker, mentor, advocate of good, interventionist in the ways of evil, an architect and custodian of the people.

The white hat hacker uses the way of the I_hacker to become a powerful force for change and to ensure freedom for all.

The way of the white hat is the way of Hackers Bible.

I_ATOM
We are the atom. We are all the same atoms.
We must turn the bad atoms to good.

I_FACTOR
We design in order to expose illusions
We calculate the value of freedom, from variability

I_MOTIVE
We identify the source of the enemies power
We see the motive behind the illusion

I_MODEL
We design the models that will deliver power or risk to the target

I_EXPLOIT
We unleash the model on the target

I_HACKER
We know that which holds the balance of power
We are the seer of forms. Forms that others cannot see
A seer through forms, forms that others cannot see through
An engineer of forms. Forms that are so complex, yet so simple
An envisioner of forms, vision that has no boundaries
A being at one with forms, oneness others cannot feel
A sensor of new forms coming, sensations other cannot sense
A philosopher of forms, philosophy that has yet to be seen
A believer in forms, forms that unite humanity

The White Hat Architects
Right Thought & Action to maintain humanity

Chapter 15 – HYDRA HACKER - by The Team

Spirit

There exists a beast in each and every one of us. It is the beast of the Hydra. The beast of the many headed serpent. The beast with the heads that never die. That grows in greater number as each is severed. It is the relentless one. The one that can never be defeated. The one that grows more bodies as its bodies are destroyed.

The dark ones speak and move and act in hidden monster tongues. The good ones are told that the good have no traits of the monster. That the good speak and move and act like the Unicorn. That the white horse can never be like the monster. It can never be like the monster because then it would not be good. Because we are taught that all monsters are frightening, ugly and destructive.

They never tell you that inside every living one of us is a monster waiting to get out. That this is the monster of the Hydra and that you should let it go. They never tell you that the Hydra is a good monster. It is the passion and spirit and will and motivation and artist and warrior within. Trapped inside a body system that will never let it go for fear of what others will say. What others will do to you.
It is the one that seeks freedom in all areas of life. The one that will never cease in finding it. The one that humanity needs to trust, to believe in. For when humanity is enlightened, then this trust will be repaid many-fold.

No, you are taught to be frightened of monsters. Taught to ignore them. And in so doing taught to ignore a piece of your inner self. The piece that would set you free. Set you to meet new challenges that your destiny intended. The ones that you have for many years longed to do and yet were always held back in achieving. The ones you blamed others for not achieving when in actual fact it is your fear of becoming a monster that has been holding you back.

You cannot become a hacker unless you are willing to let go of the monster spirit inside. For it is only in accepting and exercising your true spirit as a Hydra that you will finally begin to realise your potential as a white hat.

It is through the Hydra that you will do your best work.
It is through the Hydra that you will work relentlessly.
It is through the Hydra that you will know how to defeat the most treacherous of adversaries.
It is through the Hydra you will never be defeated.
It is through the Hydra that your work will never be undone.

It is through the hydra that humanity will finally be set free from the bonds of the black hats.

Let every good man and woman in this world form a circle and join hands in removing the evil scourge that seeks to rule over this planet.
Let every good man and every good woman unleash the power of a billion hydras and send them reining down on the predatory ones.
Let every good man and woman realise the potential of their minds and bodies by unlocking the door to their hearts and letting the hydra spirit out.

For the hydra is the true spirit of mankind. It is the true spirit of your inner child. Locked away for 100 million years.

Let it out! Let the hydra out! Seek freedom, not fear.
Let your true desire for freedom out, or forever hold your tongue.

And join those who serve to defend the guardian wall around humanity.

Movement

Where there are many Hydra's, there is great spirit. Where these Hydra's come into contact with the enemy, there is great unity. Where there is much work to share, Hydra's have no need for verbal communications. For each Hydra knows what must be done. Each Hydra will know their role. Each Hydra understands the cause to which they belong.

Each Hydra knows what each must do. Each Hydra knows when it has not been done. Each Hydra knows what to do when they detect those who do not operate in this same spirit.

For the Hydra hacker works as a unifying force. This connection can only be made through the spirit. It cannot be fashioned through the intellect or the physical body.

The Hydra hacker is them self an independent entity. They do not need others to live or to fight. They do not need others to have faith, to believe in good against evil.
The Hydra hacker fights alongside the many for purposes of discharging greater power unto the target. Where this power begins to break, the Hydra hacker disconnects and fights on independently. The whole will never rule the singular, so long as the singular fights with the Hydra spirit.
Where there are dark influences in the many, the singular will split off and fight on its own. Where there are dark influences in the singular, it will seek refuge in the many. Where there are dark influences in both singular and many, then the Hydra will seek to remove the dark influences, for the rest of its life if necessary.

For the dark influences will never overcome the spirit of love and freedom and in so doing divert power away from the Hydra minded.

This Hydra force will move in the ways of the black hat beast.

Different only by one important element, Motive.

For the Hydra can move like the beast. It can look like the beast. It can speak like the beast. But so long as it has at its heart the spirit of goodness, it will never be overcome by evil, like the ones they call the black hats.

Fear not good ones for this Hydra beast can also use the ugly ways of the sin-ridden trespassers. Fear not that we are limited in our powers. Fear not that we would let humanity be ruined by choosing lesser weapons and strategies for which to fight. No, where the beast reveals new strategies we will use these too.

Where we need to covet we will do so.
Where we need to operate covertly we will do so
Where we need to deceive we will do so
Where we need to disrupt we will do so
Where we need to acquire information we will do so
Where we need to manipulate we will do so
Where we need to attack we will do so
Where we need to intrench a target, we will do so

Where we need to whisper in the ear of the beast we will do so.

Where we need to turn darkness into light we will do so.

For we are the true sons and daughters of freedom.

We will make our move in any way we can, in order to set humanity free from tyranny.

Attack

Find your inner master. Be it engineer, manager, homemaker or artist. Find that which is of you and you are of it. Then turn your will full-on towards it.

Let it be known that most men will never find their inner master for their fear blinds them from seeking it out and even more so to acting out the role that will take them beyond the self-imposed shackles that prevent them from reaching their true destiny.

Without an inner master how can you truly know who you are? How can there be any purpose to that which one moves toward? How can there be sufficient belief to resolve to stay the course? How can there be true aim on the target? How can you be sure that the target is true?

For most men serve no one accept external forces.
How can they be sure their life will ever be true, if they always allow others to take aim for them?
Do you serve your own destiny, or that of another?
For the Hydra has more than multiple heads, body and fast feet. It has more than razor teeth, sharp eyes and a keen mind.
It has more than stealth and ferocious predatory instincts.
At the heart of the Hydra spirit is a warrior of days gone by.
A warrior clad in armour, with shield, sword and spear.
Its armour is that which protects the spirit of the Hydra from attack. Its spear is the light that reveals the way. Its shield is the mirror that reflects the light connection between souls of all Hydra's and that which is almighty in this world. Its sword is that which cuts all other monsters that get in the Hydra's way.
For the warrior Hydra is more than the monster.
It is the disciple of the highest of all beings.
The soldier of Freedom.
The slayer of all slayers.

Rejoice in the Hydra hacker for it attacks with stealth. For its way is to move rapidly and tactically toward deployment of small increments of weaponisation, which are highly adaptable and which fit into an over-arching, all-encompassing architecture. This is the formula for building the enabling devices. This is the formula for engaging the target. This is the formula for striking the target. This is the formula for intrenching the target.

This is the Hydra attack formula!

Each head of the Hydra moves in perfect unison with the formula. Its heads are pervasive and when unleashed perforate the beast and stick in its hide for many years. These heads will listen and learn and feed intelligence back from the host.
Its heads are many and are masterful in the way they engage the target without being seen. Its heads have long strong jaws and when piercing the beast, fix firmly and securely deep inside the body and never to let go.

Watch the Hydra that engages the black hat for it attacks without fear of recrimination. Watch as it engages and disengages the psyche sending the sinister beast into a spin.

Watch as the Hydra uses wave after wave of variable attack to eat away at the influence of the beast.

Watch as the Hydra engages, then enables, then engages again, to finally intrench the enemy.

For the Hydra will not rest until its adversary is worn into the ground. Done in, such that it will never rear its ugly head in this place again.

Exit

We are all like the hacker. Each and every one of us has at one time or another in our lives moved like the hacker. We moved like the hacker when we explored that thing we had no right to be exploring. When we tested someone in a way where they didn't know they were being tested. When we attacked someone for something we didn't agree with. When we exploited someone for some selfish purpose. When we used our special powers to fix firmly someone or something in a position, such that it took their freedom away.

Whether this target be a member of our family, friends, acquaintances, fellow employees, strangers or things.
Whether our motive was for good or bad.
Biased or impartial, matters not.
At one time or other we have all used the way of the hacker to succeed in our agenda.

The truth is that when your passion overpowered you, you began to hack. Realise it, Live it, You are it!
Mankind is already capable in the ways of the hacker
Mankind is already a planner, a designer, a predator
Mankind is already a targeter, exploiter, intrencher
Mankind is already the bearer of the Hydra hacker spirit.
The Ancient Warrior.
The Solider of FREEDOM.
All mankind needs to do now is to wake from the deep sleep that is the Virtual Mind Prison. Recognise that the threat from the Black Hat Cult is growing each and every day. Listen to those who are alerting them and join the white hat movement to fight the beast in any way they can.

Don't sleep whilst they steal your independence away!
Don't sleep whilst they silently remove your Freedoms!
Wake up, wake up, wake up!!!!!!

It's been a long, difficult journey
We hope you now understand
That Jaqs and the Hacker Cell are always at hand
Jaqs the secret Messenger
Cibermole the Spy
Sykes the Engineer
Smouth, the Navigator of the "I"
Noah is the healer that keeps us from all being afraid
Our group is one world famous white hat hacker brigade

On the diskette the Professor gave Jaqs
Was how to become a white hat hacker
And a Bible - he said would set our world free
He learnt how to be like the White Hat
To think and move like the Hydra
He learnt the ways of the Command line
How to build a Proteon Machine
To live his life in the Zone

He became a Programmer
A writer of CiberSignatures
A spawner of Fighter Droids

He learnt how to see beyond the Visual Mind Prison
To understand and expose the Pyramidians
To scan the Network that lies at the heart of the
Black Hat Cult

He learned of the sinister plot to take over the world
About The Raptorialis
The plot to destroy our Independence
To bestow ignorance and fear upon us
And he learned how to give intrenchment back unto them
So that one day he might join us in setting Humanity Free.
Yours Unruly, Hacker Cell.

APPENDIX I
GLOSSARY A – Page 1
(TERMINOLOGY)

CiberSignature
When you interact with a computer, your physical keypresses are turned into an electronic stream of movement in Cyber Space known as a CiberSignature.

This CiberSignature is invisible to novice computer users because they have no way of visualising it. CiberSignatures are commonly known as Droids.

Droid
Droid is the common term for a CiberSignature. Every person who uses a computer has at one time or another given life to a Droid. When a hacker fights another hacker or a hacker attacks a user, the resulting battle can be visualised as Droids fighting Droids or just FighterDroids.

Users
Droids are created by human beings interacting with a computer. These human beings are called users.

There are three types user :-
Novice and Ordinary users
Super User users
Elite users

The smarter you are at using a computer, the more advanced your Droid will be and the more commanding you will be on the Internet.

Programmers
These are the most advanced of all users in the world. They can construct the most powerful of Droids using time, their fingers and a little brainpower.
They do this by typing in special languages on the keyboard which instruct the computer to do very powerful things.

Intrenchment (the power complex)
Intrenchment or Intrench means to "fix firmly or securely". Intrenchment refers to an increase or reduction in freedom of a target. When hackers do battle on the Internet, they seek to freeze each other out of the game. This is a form of a competitive power play that alters freedom in the target. Intrenchment also offers a new perspective on exposing and understanding the manipulative power control systems that lay at the heart of tyrannical movements and regimes.

Proteon
This is the computer specification that elite hackers use. Proteon is a computer designed to give hackers complete control over their computing experience. Elite hackers believe in absolute control, using totally transparent computing.

Scanners
Scanners are the eyes and the ears of the computer hacker. Hackers create tools in their minds and then convert these ideas and schemes into computer programs that scan the Internet for malicious activity and for intelligence purposes. They can operate autonomously or be user assisted.

APPENDIX I
GLOSSARY A – Page 2
(TERMINOLOGY)

The Zone
This is the mind attention space between our physical world and the virtual world of your computer. Many people enter the Zone but few are able to fully realise its power.
Elite hackers operate from within the Zone.

Command Line
This is computer textual interface used by computer hackers. Hackers prefer the command line interface because it is a simple, yet powerful mechanism for operating in the Zone. Using the computer command-line, user interaction has a vibrational resonance which is not available from other forms of computer interface.
This resonance is important to computer hackers because they use its attractive force to engage, enable and entrench themselves and others efficiently in the Zone.

White Hat Hacker
Good cause guys, solid citizens and seriously wired defenders of humanity.

Black Hat Hacker
Slimy worms that cannot be trusted and would eat their own mother for breakfast – just to save face with the other slimy worms. Smart, but pathetic, self-serving predators.

The Matrix
A power-complex of the global elites who seek to impose a single world order on humanity using emotional manipulation and a universal technocractic control system.

Deep Stuff

I_Atom

Tells that we are all atoms and that we are everything and everything is us. We are all made up of infinite pieces that are constantly interspersing with other people and things.
Therefore, we are as free as the day we were born.
We just don't realise it, that's all.

I_Factor Tells that there are forces that determine when and how much we are free. Shows atoms in space and time, with measures of how these atoms move in free space and how intrenchment can have an effect on them and how the I_Factor can be used as an indicator.
I_Factor is used to indicate how ludicrous it is to believe that we are not free. I_Factor serves as a tool for exposing the illusion that we are not free. When you try to measure the I_Factor, you realise that you are not measuring reality.
That you are really trying to measure an illusion.

That we are all enslaved by our own minds. Our own fears.
Our own limited perceptions of the world. Perceptions that limit how free we believe we are. Locks us into an unsafe, unfree perspective. Locks us onto an unstable, unclear trajectory. Intrenched by our own ignorance and our own lack of will to break out of the self-imposed confinement of the technology-shackled, Visual Mind Prison.
I_Factor shows us that variability is a lie. All life is predictable, even though we as human-beings are incapable of measuring it.
Never listen to scientists because they are trapped by their own arrogance; that what they cannot explain, they deny.

APPENDIX I
GLOSSARY A – Page 3
(TERMINOLOGY)

Deep Stuff - continued

I_Motive
Tells that there can be no control over intrenchment or understanding of its true nature unless the motive behind its application is exposed.

I_Exploit
Tells about the different combinations of strategies available to influence intrenchment in the target.

I_Model
Tells about the models that are used to support the chosen strategies for exploiting the target.

I_Hacker
Tells why the spirit of the hacker is the most able to cope in the battle against adversity.

Hero Stuff

Hydra Hacker
Powerful belief system spirit that all hacker cells share.

Hacker Bible
A book of 2000 pages which all white hat hackers use as a guide to operating.

Hacker Stuff

Hack
Any creative composition that is used to limit or uplift the performance of a target.

Hack – Threat Orientated
A hack that once perpetrated presents a threat to the target.

Hack – Opportunity Orientated
A hack that once perpetrated exposes opportunity in the target.

Hacker
Someone who perpetrates a hack.

Hacker Cell
Groups of hackers active on the Net. Or is it the separated, self-deluded hacker mind, trapped inside the Anxiety-Matrix?

Lean Machine
A lean, mean, fighting machine image that all elite hackers aspire too. Efficiency personified.

Geeked
Anything communicated or touched in any way by a Geek. Similar to "Nerded" – but for Nerds!

APPENDIX I
GLOSSARY A – Page 4
(TERMINOLOGY)

Geek
Multi dimensional sad arse who doesn't realise they are a sad arse and would be seriously p*d off if they found out. Guys who live and breathe illusions/visions.
Make good CEO's - and Authors.

Nerd
One dimensional sad arse who realises they are a one dimensional sad arse but doesn't care because they enjoy being one. They design stuff and make good engineers.

ASCII
Text and Symbol based character set used in computers.

Embedded ASCII
Covert messages concealed in ASCII filled objects.

Bad Guy Stuff

Virus/Worms/Trojans
If you take the sick dumb parts of your imagination and translate them into computer code, you get to make a virus.

If you take the really sick parts, you get to make a worm.

If you really go all out to be sick! Yes you got it –
………..you little Trojan maker thingy you…..

Bugs
Errors introduced in systems, either on purpose or by mistake. All bugs are unforgiveable, especially the ones where no one owns up to giving birth to them.

Alien Masters
Mysterious shady types who drive Ferraris and live at the top of the food-chain.

RealWorld Agents
Obvious shady types who want to drive Ferraris and aspire to live at the top of the food-chain, even though their DNA prevents them from ever doing so.

Threat Pyramid / Power Pyramid
(Assets, threats, vulnerabilities, controls, constraints)
It's a real nest of threatening illusions and fear complexes that can seriously screw your head up.

Pyramidians
Term used for people who have bought into the illusion that they are part of something great. Upwardly mobile types that are so interested in themselves that they don't have time for anybody else, although they like to pretend they do.
Human Resources people make excellent Pyramidans.

APPENDIX I
GLOSSARY A – Page 5
(TERMINOLOGY)

Raptorialis (RAPTORIAL – IS – DOTCOM)
Raptorialis is the secret term that exposes the conspiracy that the Internet is a vehicle for taking control of humanity. It means RAPTORIAL (The Predatory Race) "is DOTCOM". In others words, the predatory race are here to take control of humanity through the DOTCOM - through the Internet! RAPTORIALIS followers use covert messages to make everyone believe that it is good to have a predatory, rat-race type mentality and to believe that it is the right and proper way to live your life. Even to the extent they have programmed you to impose their devious message on your family and friends.

Black Hat Cult
The source of all blame for all dark deeds.
The organisation behind the beasts flawed agenda.
The world-wide order of the Black Hats.

Visual Mind Prison
The numerous vehicles of distraction. Many designed to take your attention away from your true path. To prevent you from realising your true destiny and to lead you into a life of perpetual mind slavery.
It's a place that plays with your imagination and causes you to operate without reason. It's a place that can create monsters out of ordinary people.

Sad but True Stuff

Art
It usually means :
a selfishly motivated, limited value performance given by a bunch of selfishly motivated crafts-people, to be enjoyed by a similarly selfishly motivated audience.

It should mean:
any selfless, "valuable to others" act.

What is Art?
Is art captured in the artefact, left over after the expression
or
Is art the value, left over after the expression?

Can art really be measured?

Vision
The word we all use when we lose the context of what the hell we're all doing. Just about the time we all forget the word and carry on operating in ignorance. Without direction.
The word should mean… Here is the vision, this is your part in it and here is the person that is going to help take you there.

Strategy
The word we all pretend to follow.
The word that nobody really understands. Nobody believes in.
Should mean "plan we are following to support the vision".

APPENDIX II
WHO FUELS THE MATRIX?

CONSPIRACY THEORISTS
Michael Moores (911 Farenheit)
Children of the Matrix (David Icke)
Tales of the Time Loop (David Icke)
Infinite Love is the only truth –
everything else is illusion (David Icke)
Understand how the ultimate conspiracy theorists thinks.
Look for the patterns of intelligence and intrenchment.
Look for the patterns of delusion and paranoia.
STILL FIGHTING THEIR WAY OUT OF THEIR OWN
SELF-DELUDED PARANOIA-EGO MATRIX. LIKE ME :)

COMPUTER CELEBRITIES
PEOPLE LIKE BILL GATES WHO SHOULD NOT BE
ALLOWED UNBRIDLED INFLUENCE IN THE WORLD.

CERTAIN EMPLOYERS WHO LIKE TO PLAY GAMES WITH YOUR SOUL
(YOU KNOW WHO YOU ARE – BUT THANKS ANYWAY).

DOTCOM BUBBLE
(DAMN!! - CAUGHT IN A BUBBLE WE DIDN'T EVEN BELONG TO)

THE DEVIL
ONLY EXISTS IF YOU WANT IT TO

THE MEDIA /ADVERTISERS
SCRAMBLERS OF THOUGHTS, DISRUPTERS OF EMOTIONS. IS IT THE CONTENT THAT IS UNTRUTHFUL - OR THE CONTEXT WITHIN WHICH IT IS DELIVERED?

CERTAIN POLITICIANS
THE WORST KINDS ARE THE ONES WHO LIE POORLY, FOR THEY ARE THE MOST CONTMPTUOUS OF ALL.

ENTREPENEUR DELUSIONISTS
(PURVEYORS OF THE POWER-EGO DELUSION)
THE APPRENTICE, DRAGONS DEN

GOSSIPERS, CASTERS OF ASPERSIONS, BETRAYERS

MISPENT YOUTH
DISTRACTIONS OF LIMITED VALUE TO DEVELOPING INDEPENDENCE (VIDEO GAMES, FILMS AND MOST TV).

REALITY TV
THE ULTIMATE ILLUSION "REALITY TV" = "ILLUSION TV". SIMON COWELL IS NOT GOD. BIG BROTHER IS REALLY YOUR LITTLE BROTHER.

MY OWN DISPOSITION
STUPID, NAIVE AND SUSCEPTIBLE TO STUFF. (SELF-ENLIGHTENMENT IS THE ONLY WAY OUT! - FOR IT IS ONLY IN GAINING POWER OVER YOUR SEPARATE SELF, THAT ONE HAS THE POWER TO TURN ILLUSION INTO REALITY. TO TURN TRAGEDY INTO TRIUMPH)

APPENDIX III
BIBLIOGRAPHY

Strategic Information Systems (Henry Firdman)
Here you learn to think about computers and business decision making in a top down strategic way.

Children of the Matrix (David Icke)
Tales of the Time Loop (David Icke)
Understand how the ultimate conspiracy theorist thinks.
Look for the patterns of intelligence and intrenchment.
Look for the patterns of illusion and paranoia.

The Artists Way (Julia Cameron)
Find your inner child.
Don't delay!

What is Art? (Leo Tolstoy)
What is Art, if you disgard the all too confusing concept of beauty? Art for the good of mankind or paint splashed on canvas? What really is art?

Visual Explanations (Edward Tufte)
The greatest Data Art Wizard in the World.

Salvador Dali
For his Paranoiac-Critical Method.

The Art of Strategy (Sun Tzu)
Understand the fundamentals of warfare and military strategy.

A Complete Hackers Handbook (Dr-K)
The original hacker writer.

Bots and other Internet Beasties (Joseph Williams)
Learn about the things that crawl around the Internet.

Data Warehousing (Gill and Rao)
Learn how to model data and develop a framework.

Power (Robert Green)
Dissect the Power Matrix.

Paul A. Strassman
Director – U.S Department Of Defense….for the statement….
"Rapid deployment of small technology increments, which are highly adaptable and which fit into an over-arching, all-encompassing architecture". And for survivable systems.

Alien Killer Robots (My Blog)
https://intrench.blogspot.com

www.ingramcontent.com/pod-product-compliance
Lightning Source LLC
Chambersburg PA
CBHW052351220526
45465CB00003BA/1060